LIKE A PELTING RAIN

THE MAKING OF THE MODERN MIND

By
Roland Cap Ehlke

1517 Publishing

Like a Pelting Rain: The Making of the Modern Mind
© 2018 Roland Cap Ehlke

All rights reserved. No part of this publication may be reproduced, distributed, or transmitted in any form or by any means, including photocopying, recording, or other electronic or mechanical methods, without the prior written permission of the publisher, except in the case of brief quotations embodied in critical reviews and certain other noncommercial uses permitted by copyright law. For permission requests, write to the publisher at the address below.

Published by:
1517 Publishing
PO Box 54032
Irvine, CA 92619-4032

Cover art by Roland Cap Ehlke, *Summer Rain*.
Cover design and book layout by Paul Roland Ehlke.
Special thanks to Dr. Angus Menuge for the chapter "Intellectual Themes of the Reformation."

Printed in the United States of America

Publisher's Cataloging-In-Publication Data
(Prepared by The Donohue Group, Inc.)

Names: Ehlke, Roland Cap.
Title: Like a pelting rain : the making of the modern mind / by Roland Cap Ehlke.
Description: Irvine, CA : 1517 Publishing, [2018] | Previously published: Milwaukee : Ehlkeworks Publishing, 2013. | Includes bibliographical references and index.
Identifiers: ISBN 9781945978203 (softcover) | ISBN 9781945978234 (ebook)
Subjects: LCSH: Christianity and culture—History. | Aesthetics—Religious aspects—Christianity. | Aesthetics—History. | Intellectual life—Religious aspects—Christianity.
Classification: LCC BR115.C8 E45 2018 (print) | LCC BR115.C8 (ebook) | DDC 261—dc23

"The Gospel is rather like a pelting rain that hurries on from place to place. What it hits it hits; what it misses it misses. But it does not return nor stay in one place; the sun and heat come after it and lick it up. Experience . . . teaches us that in no section of the world has the Gospel remained pure and unadulterated beyond the memory of . . . man."[1]

Martin Luther

---

[1] Martin Luther, *What Luther Says: An Anthology*, Ewald M. Plass, compiler (St. Louis: Concordia, 1959), vol. 2, 573.

CONTENTS

Introduction: Aesthetic Grounding — 7

Part 1. The Age of Reformation 1450–1650 — 9
Renaissance and Reformation — 9
The English Reformation — 12
Intellectual Themes of the Reformation — 14
Ongoing Reformation — 18

Part 2. The Age of Enlightenment 1650–1800 — 25
The Rise of Deism — 25
Apostles of Deism — 31
The Troubled Eighteenth Century — 36
Women Writers — 41
The Kantian Revolution — 46
William Carey and the Expansion of Christianity — 50

Part 3. The Age of Romanticism 1800–1850 — 55
The Early Romantics — 55
The Later Romantics — 60
American Romanticism: Ralph Waldo Emerson — 67
American Romanticism: Edgar Allan Poe — 72

Part 4. The Victorian Age 1850–1900 — 79
Charles Dickens: Man in the Middle — 79
Alfred Lord Tennyson and the Spirit of the Age — 84
Charles Darwin and the Theory of Evolution — 88
Victorian Voices — 94
American Excursion: Sea of Light and Spirit — 100
Truth and Art at the End of the Nineteenth Century — 105

Part 5. The Age of Modernism and Beyond 1900–the Present — 111
Revolt of the Soul: William Butler Yeats — 111
German Excursion: From Babel to Berlin — 118
The Birth of the Modern: The Nurturers — 123
The Birth of the Modern: The Popularizers — 127
The Postmodern World — 133

Conclusion: The End of an Age — 143

For Study and Discussion — 145

INTRODUCTION: AESTHETIC GROUNDING

With the rise of Christianity and its establishment as the religion of the Roman Empire and, later, as the heart of the Holy Roman Empire, European life came to center around the Christian faith as espoused by the Roman Catholic Church. For centuries, all of life, aesthetics—art, music, literature—as well as science, politics, philosophy, and ethics, was linked with Christian dogma. Today that link is corroded and all but severed. *Like a Pelting Rain* traces the course of Western civilization—especially the English-speaking world—during the past five centuries. How did culture arrive at where we now are? What might we do in our time?

The poet Percy Bysshe Shelley remarked that poets—that is, the creative people—"are the unacknowledged legislators of the world." Who is more influential in shaping the attitudes of a generation? Law-makers in the halls of government, or popular artists, whether a Shelley or, in our day, the Beatles, a Madonna, the latest pop star, or . . . ?

The bond between aesthetics and faith was deep rooted. In ancient Greek literature and the Bible, the root meaning of the word aesthetics had to do with the faculty for making spiritual and moral decisions.[2] For example, St. Paul encouraged the Christians at Philippi, "And this is my prayer: that your love may abound more and more in knowledge and depth of insight [*aisthesei*]" (1:9). Religion and discernment, including in the arts, came to be linked together.

In that connection, Augustine (354-430) saw earthly beauty as far beneath spiritual concerns: "When man fell away from the unity of God the multitude of temporal forms was distributed among his carnal senses . . . he cannot find the one thing needful, a single and unchangeable nature . . . The reason why corporeal beauty is the lowest beauty is that its parts cannot all exist simultaneously. Some things give place and others succeed them."[3]

Somewhat ironically, the medieval church enlisted just such sensuous beauty to exalt the Son. Art—in the form of stained glass windows, the soaring chancels of Europe's Gothic cathedrals, the rituals of worship, and the haunting chants of monastic choirs—served to reinforce eternal truths, while helping keep the church's hold upon the masses.

---

2   See William F. Arndt and F. Wilbur Gingrich, *A Greek-English Lexicon of the New Testament and Other Early Christian Literature* (Chicago: University of Chicago Press, 1957).
3   Augustine, *On True Religion*, J. H. S. Burleigh, trans. (Chicago: Henry Regnery, 1968), 37-8.

The Reformation broke Rome's monopoly on the souls of people. It also opened the door to fresh intellectual and creative expressions, as witnessed in the hymns of Martin Luther and his followers, along with the etchings of Albrecht Dürer. Before the Reformation movement was a hundred years old, Philip Sidney wrote *An Apology for Poetry,* stating the purpose of poetry was to glorify Christ. This close connection between aesthetics and Christian faith carried into the seventeenth century, to the time of John Milton and John Bunyan.

As we trace the cultural history of the West through the centuries, the development of a gradual but definite split between culture and historic Christianity becomes obvious. Beauty and the things of the world became ends in themselves—art for art's sake. An overview of the period from the Reformation until today sheds light on the changes. Our study will trace the development of the modern mind, which by and large rejects Christian faith. Although emphasizing the aesthetic (especially representative literature), this study will also consider political, social, intellectual, and theological changes during the last five centuries. Moreover, we will see that the secularization of society was not inevitable, nor is it totally irreversible.

In a 1525 sermon, Martin Luther observed that the Gospel moves on "like a pelting rain." Indeed, earlier it had moved on from the lands where Christianity was born and first flourished—Palestine and the Middle East. Yet it is not for us to hasten that movement by fatalism or indifference. It is for each generation of Christians to treasure the Word of God before it does move on. We offer this work with the confidence that many—young and old alike—can use it as a wakeup call and as a resource for renewal. May this generation experience a return to the faith that has given life and vigor to a matchless civilization and to countless lives throughout the years and around the globe!

PART 1
THE AGE OF REFORMATION: 1450—1650

RENAISSANCE AND REFORMATION

Twilight of the Medieval World

Historians frequently refer to the Middle Ages as the millennium between A.D. 500 (the abdication of the last Roman emperor in 476, marking the end of the Ancient World) and 1500 (the time of the Renaissance, beginning of the age of European exploration, the Reformation, etc.), which ushers in the Early Modern period of history.

When Jesus said, "Give to Caesar what is Caesar's, and to God what is God's" (Matthew 22:21),[4] he laid the foundation for the separation of church and state. Nevertheless, throughout the Middle Ages, the papacy and secular powers were engaged in a struggle for supremacy. Papal power reached its zenith under Innocent III (ca. 1160-1216), who likened his pontifical authority to the light of the sun and the royal powers to the light of the moon.

The Black Death pandemic (1350), which took close to half of the population of Europe, was a harbinger of things to come. Along with the physical horror of this plague, the Roman Catholic Church was struggling with spiritual devastations. During the Avignon papacy (1309-1377)—known as the Babylonian Captivity of the Church—the church's authority was undermined, with French popes residing in Avignon, which would become a center of corruption and prostitution. The forty-year Western Schism that followed saw the papacy split between two rival popes (Rome and Avignon), and for a brief time three (Pisa). The Council of Constance (1415) ended the schism with the election of Pope Martin V. Alongside simony, the buying of ecclesiastical offices (see Acts 8:18-24) ran the practice of nepotism, showing favoritism to friends and relatives, as evidenced by the Pope Alexander VI (1492-1503), who used his ecclesiastical power to advance his illegitimate children.

---

[4] Scripture quotation is from Robert Hoerber, ed., *Concordia Self-Study Bible: New International Version* (St. Louis: Concordia, 1986). Subsequent Bible quotations are from this edition.

Reformers arose across Europe. In England, John Wyclif (ca. 1330-84)—"the Morning Star of the Reformation"—sided with Scripture over tradition and translated the Bible into English. The priest John Hus (1373-1415), a disciple of Wyclif, brought reforming ideas to Bohemia. The Italian Dominican monk Girolamo Savonarola (1452-98) spoke out against the materialism and immorality of his day. Both Hus and Savonarola were put to death.

The fall of Constantinople in 1453 to the Muslim Ottoman Turks marked the collapse of Christendom's 1000-year bastion. Nevertheless, refugees from the city brought with them to Italy ancient texts. Around 1450, the invention of the printing press, credited to the German Johannes Gutenberg, opened new vistas to the exchange of ideas and ushered in the age of modern mass communication. Physically, European horizons expanded with the voyages of Christopher Columbus and other explorers. Already by the end of the Middle Ages, in technology and other areas, the Christian nations of Europe "greatly surpassed the rest of the world."[5] Yet even greater glories were soon to come. It was a time of rebirth—Renaissance.

Martin Luther Reformer

The Renaissance motto *ad fontes,* back to the sources, meant a return to the ancient languages, including the languages of the Holy Scriptures, Hebrew and Greek. Based on his studies of the Scriptures in the original languages, Martin Luther (1483-1546) came to a deep understanding of the inspired Word of God, an understanding that would transform the world.

Luther dug deeply into the Bible and on that basis developed a Christ-centered theology that reached people at their greatest need—the need to find forgiveness, peace with God, and salvation. Unlike the reformers who had gone before, Luther encompassed the whole of theology, both moral reform and doctrine. Through his study of the Bible, Luther gradually came to realize that God's righteousness is imputed to sinners. It is a free gift of God's grace, and we take hold of it simply by trusting in Christ and His perfect righteousness for our salvation.

From Luther's Christ-centered theology arose the three great pillars of the Reformation: *sola scriptura* (Scripture alone is God's revelation of salvation in Christ), *sola gratia* (grace alone, God's unmerited love in Christ, is the means to salvation), *sola fide* (faith alone is the way to receive God's grace; good works are a by-product of faith, not a way to earn God's favor).

---

5 Rodney Stark, "How Christianity (and Capitalism) Led to Science," *The Chronicle of Higher Education,* December 2, 2005, http://chronicle.com/article/How-Christianity-and/31902; see also Rodney Stark, *The Victory of Reason: How Christianity led to Freedom, Capitalism, and Western Success* (New York: Random House, 2005).

Throughout Luther's works runs the *Law-Gospel* message. The Law is that part of Scripture that points out God's demands (e.g., the Ten Commandments) and his pronouncements of judgment upon the breaking of his Law. The Law condemns everyone, since "all have sinned and fall short of the glory of God . . ." (Romans 3:23). The Gospel declares that through Christ's work—his sinless life, sacrificial death on the cross, and resurrection from the dead—sinners receive full and free forgiveness, peace with God, and salvation. As the Romans passage goes on to say, ". . . and are justified freely through the redemption that came by Christ Jesus" (3:24).

With the rediscovery of the Gospel came a plethora of subsidiary blessings. Among them was a renewed appreciation of the spiritual life. Through the printing press, Luther became the first great mass communicator. His *Ninety-five Theses*—a disputation against ecclesiastical abuses and the catalyst of the Reformation—along with ensuing writings spread throughout Europe in a way that could never have happened when manuscripts were what the word implies, hand-written and copied one at a time. The greater availability of printed material coincided with the expansion of literacy. In 1529 the Turks pushed into Eastern Europe and reached as far as Vienna, and Luther responded with classic writings on the Islamic threat.

Luther's work also advanced education for the many. The concept of vocation—we serve God in our everyday callings—brought a sense of meaning to labor. Emphasis on family life (as opposed to the medieval ideal of monasticism) was renewed. And the Christian church became a singing church, as heard in the hymns of Luther, such as the "battle hymn of the Reformation":

> A mighty fortress is our God,
> A trusty shield and weapon;
> He helps us free from every need
> That has us now o'rtaken.[6]
>
> . . . .

Spread of the Reformation

In 1521, four years after Luther posted the *Ninety-five Theses,* the Emperor Charles V declared him an outlaw. But the dam had burst, and reformers arose throughout Europe. Some went beyond Luther and advocated radical change—Thomas Münzer (1490-1525) led the Peasants' Revolt and was executed. Ulrich Zwingli (1484-1531) brought the Reformation to Switzerland but disagreed over the place of reason in rela-

---

6   Martin Luther, "A Mighty Fortress Is Our God," hymn 200 in *Christian Worship: A Lutheran Hymnal* (Milwaukee: Northwestern, 1993).

tion to Scripture, an issue that would have momentous effects over the years. The Anabaptists taught re-baptism as adults and influenced the Puritan and Baptist movements. John Knox (1514-72) brought reformation ideas to Scotland and became the father of the Presbyterian Church. Of all the other reformers, John Calvin (1509-64) was to have the most widespread influence. Born in France, he settled in Geneva, Switzerland. His voluminous *Institutes of the Christian Religion* continues to impact Reformed churches throughout the world.

THE ENGLISH REFORMATION

For all of Luther's influence, it was England, and not Germany, that would most widely affect the rise of Protestantism. Paralleling the worldwide expansion of the British Empire, English has become the international language, and no book has received such wide circulation as did the King James Version of the Bible (1611).

Henry VIII (1509-47)

On the eve of the English Reformation, the Roman Catholic Church in England was a powerful institution, with some 12,000 monks and nuns in a population of 3 million people. The church also owned a quarter of the land and was a part of everyone's life. Moreover, its ruler was a staunch defender of Roman Catholicism. For Henry's writing against Luther, Pope Leo X enthusiastically gave him the honorary title of Defender of the Faith.

In the 1530s, however, defender of the faith and pope would part ways. The split arose from Henry's desire to divorce his wife Catherine of Aragon, by whom he was unable to have a male heir, and marry Anne Boleyn, a lady of the court. The pope, Clement VII, was not inclined to grant the divorce. In 1534 Henry broke with Rome and declared himself the religious authority of England. This was the Act of Supremacy and began the English Reformation.

Amid the turmoil of the times, the Coverdale Bible (1535) became the first complete Bible printed in English.[7] Henry appointed as Archbishop of Canterbury Thomas Cranmer (1489-1556), who would greatly influence the English church. Henry died a Catholic in doctrine and practice, and in 1547 England much of Catholicism remained in place. Yet the picture is more complicated, as Henry left his son in the hands of Protestant protectors.

---

7   Andrew Sanders, *The Short Oxford History of English Literature* (Oxford: Clarendon Press, 1996), 85

The Theology of the English Reformation

Roman Catholic Tradition

Even after Henry's split with Rome, English Catholicism remained strong in many ways. During the time of Henry, the Church of England continued to use liturgies in Latin. The *Six Articles* of 1539 (repealed in 1547) for a time reestablished Catholic doctrine, such as transubstantiation and clerical celibacy (even Archbishop Cranmer had to give up his wife for a time). The English transition away from Catholicism, then, was a gradual process.

Lutheran Form

Despite Henry's antipathy to Luther, several key factors linked England and Germany in the early years of the Reformation. William Tyndale trained at Oxford and Cambridge, but also studied with Luther in Wittenberg. His 1525 translation of the Bible into English was printed in Germany and became a model for the King James Bible of 1611.[8] The prominent figure in the Lutheran-English conferences of 1536 and 1538, Robert Barnes, spent three years there.

Calvinist Rationalism

In 1529, Martin Luther, Philip Melanchthon, and other German theologians met with Ulrich Zwingli, Martin Bucer, and other Swiss and southern German reformers at the castle of Marburg to try to establish unity among the various branches of reformers. Two facets of the meeting relate closely to what was or would be taking place in England.

The first has to do with Zwingli's position at Marburg, where he met with Luther. Although the two parties agreed on a number of issues, they were unable to agree on the meaning of Christ's words in the Eucharist. Zwingli's side advanced the argument that a body could not be in two places at once and that Christ was using a figure of speech. Luther had written *Hoc est corpus meum* ("This is my body") on the table where they sat, pulled back the tablecloth to reveal the words, and demanded what figure of speech was involved. The issue of rationalism lay behind this stalemate. The position of Zwingli and his followers has been expressed in the words, *Finitum non est capax infiniti*—the finite is not capable of containing the infinite. For Luther "in Christ the finite human nature has indeed proved itself capable of the infinite Godhead."[9]

---

8   See Lewis Foster, *Selecting a Translation of the Bible* (Cincinnati: Standard, 1978), 20.
9   Francis Pieper, *Christian Dogmatics* (St. Louis; Concordia, 1951), vol. 2, 261.

The other significant aspect of Marburg was that one of the participants was Martin Bucer of Strasbourg. A mediator, conciliator, and a Zwinglian at heart, Bucer tried to bring the two sides together. During the reign of Edward VI, Bucer was invited to England, where he gave Cranmer advice regarding the 1552 prayer book. In the section on communion, the wording was ambiguous, allowing for either a representational or actual presence of Christ's body and blood.

Zwingli's name was soon to be overshadowed by that of another theologian who found his home in Switzerland, John Calvin. Although French, he settled in Geneva. This reformer, who had studied under Bucer, was to have an immense impact on English theology. Calvinist theology is reflected in the circumspect wording of the *Thirty-Nine Articles,* in which any reference to a real physical presence of Christ in the sacrament is vague. Calvinism is evident in the general tendency toward rationalism that would mark English thought.

Edward VI (1547-53)

Edward VI was only twelve years old when he succeeded his father. His reign is more the story of his tutors or advisors than of his own views. During the brief reign of the boy king, Protestantism established a more secure beachhead on British shores. The year 1549 saw the publication of the first edition of the *Book of Common Prayer*. While retaining certain Catholic elements, English worship was taking on a separate and distinct life of its own. The *Forty-Two Articles,* completed shortly before his death, discredited the Catholic doctrines of Roman primacy, transubstantiation, and the mass as a sacrifice.[10] These articles, largely the work of Cranmer, became the basis for the *Thirty-Nine Articles* that under Queen Elizabeth would definitively shape Anglican theology.

INTELLECTUAL THEMES OF THE REFORMATION

Christian Humanism

The Protestant Reformation was part of sweeping reforms in education. While "humanism" is associated today with a secular worldview, a distinctively Christian humanism arose as part of the rebirth (renaissance) of learning in the universities of Northern Italy in the late fourteenth century, which upheld the value of classical sources alongside a deep concern for theology. At the University of Wittenberg there was a particular emphasis on the value of science, at that time called "natural philosophy." There was also an explosion of interest in astronomy.

---

10 A. G. Dickens, *The English Reformation* (New York: Schocken, 1964), 253.

Reformation and the Rise of Science

While the scientific profession is held in high regard today, it was not easily accepted by universities in the sixteenth century, the beginning of the "scientific revolution." At that time, there were only three recognized vocations: medicine, law, and theology.

Catholic theology had drawn a distinction between the "spiritual estate" of the clergy, devoted directly to God, and the inferior "temporal estate" of the laity who had to *add* acts of religious devotion onto their purely worldly activities. One of the great breakthroughs of Luther was to see that this distinction was unbiblical. When Paul became an evangelist, he nevertheless continued with his tent-making, and told other Christians to remain in the station where they were called (1 Corinthians 7:20), as a way to serve others and witness their faith. Luther concluded, "All Christians are truly of the spiritual estate, and there is no difference among them except that of office."[11] This was the priesthood of all believers (1 Peter 2:9).

The other factor that helped to legitimize science was the recovery of an ancient idea, that God had communicated to human beings in two books, the Bible (the book of God's Word, which disclosed His plan of salvation) and nature (the book of God's works, which testified to His eternal qualities [Romans 1:18-20]). This meant there was a legitimate area of study which focused on God's works in the natural world. The famous Lutheran astronomer Johannes Kepler (1571-1630) saw nature as a kind of temple and science as an act of worship.[12]

This study of nature was a departure from the scholastic concern with the opinions of ancient authorities. This shift from studying books about nature to studying nature herself depended on another breakthrough of the Reformation, a revolution in hermeneutics.[13] While not denying the spiritual value of allegories, the reformers came to see that the only firm ground for doctrine was the literal (historical-grammatical) meaning of the text. The same applied to the natural world.

They also came to realize that there was no substitute for empirical study. A sovereign God was free to inscribe whatever order he deemed best in nature. The scholastic idea of *anticipating* nature in terms of preconceptions about its essences had to be rejected in favor of the more humble task of *interpreting* what God had done. This is why Kepler was content to say the astronomer's job is to think God's thoughts *after him*, and why Tycho Brahe (1546-1601) was willing to spend years of painstaking work in his observatory.

---

11 Martin Luther, "To the Christian Nobility of the German Nation (1520)," in *Three Treatises* (Philadelphia: Fortress, 1970), 12.
12 Peter Harrison, "Priests of the Most High God, with Respect to the Book of Nature," in ed. Angus Menuge, *Reading God's World: The Scientific Vocation* (St. Louis: Concordia, 2004), 70.
13 Peter Harrison, *The Bible, Protestantism and the Rise of Modern Science* (New York: Cambridge University Press, 1998).

Perhaps the most important figure in making astronomy an acceptable part of the Wittenberg curriculum was Phillip Melanchthon (1487-1560). Despite his interest in astrology, Melanchthon saw astronomy as providing evidence of God's providential care of the world. To the modern secular mind, there is no link between moral laws (if they are accepted at all) and laws of physics. But for Melanchthon and other Lutheran thinkers, both kinds of law were subsumed under the idea of natural law, and the laws of physics had apologetic value in providing a model of orderly human existence in society.[14] This understanding of natural law was vital to the Lutheran response to the Anabaptists, who rejected both church and civil hierarchies, fueling unrest and anarchy. Melanchthon was confident that an appeal to natural law would prevail; he accepted a common belief of the time which supported the natural knowledge of God. This was the idea that human beings were endowed with a "natural light" (a remnant of the image of God) that enabled them to intuit the truth of clearly presented mathematical and moral principles.

Reconciling the Two Books

The well-known cliché that Luther was anti-science is rather difficult to reconcile with the fact that under his direction, the University of Wittenberg was a center of scientific advancement.

According to a remark often attributed to Luther (and appearing in "Table Talk"), Luther rejected the proposal of Nicolaus Copernicus (1473-1543) that the earth revolved around the sun (the heliocentric hypothesis) because it was incompatible with Scripture. Anthony Lauterbach, a dinner guest of Luther's, recalls the conversation.[15] On the basis of this, it has been argued that the University of Wittenberg suppressed astronomical study and that it mistreated the mathematicians Georg Joachim Rheticus (1514-75) and Erasmus Reinhold (1511-53) because of their Copernican sympathies. "[N]owhere were the facts confirming the Copernican theory more carefully kept out of sight than at Wittenberg— the University of Luther and Melanchthon...."[16]

The best commentators have shown convincingly that this analysis is entirely erroneous, for a number of reasons. First, it is not even clear that Luther actually said what was attributed to him, as "Table Talk." Second, even if he did, no such comments can be found in any of Luther's serious published work, and everyone, including Luther, is liable to make some incautious remarks over the years when enjoying a beer with friends. Thirdly, Luther allegedly made the remark in 1539, four

---

14   Peter Barker, "Astronomy, Providence, and the Lutheran Contribution to Science," Menuge, *Reading God's World*, 164.

15   Theodore G. Tappert, editor and translator, "Table Talk," *Luther's Works*, vol. 54, (Philadelphia: Fortress Press, 1967), 358-9.

16   Andrew Dickson White, *A History of the Warfare of Science with Theology in Christendom* (New York: D. Appleton, 1929), vol. 1, 128-9.

years before the appearance of Copernicus's work, *On the Revolutions of the Heavenly Spheres*, so any remarks would have been based on speculation, not serious study.

At a more fundamental level, however, most scientists of the time agreed with the earth-centered (geocentric) model, not only because it agreed with common sense (the earth does not appear to be moving), but also because there was no conclusive scientific evidence of the earth's rotation. The facts confirming the Copernican theory simply had not been established at the time. And contrary to a widely held urban legend, it is not even true that Copernicus's system was simpler than Ptolemy's.[17] Luther, who had himself studied astronomy, was not reactionary, but simply a person of his times in accepting the scientific consensus that the Earth was stationary.

Luther and Melanchthon allowed the study of Copernicus's ideas at Wittenberg because they embraced a sophisticated philosophy of science, according to which one could accept a mathematical model for its accuracy of prediction, without committing to it as a literal description of objective reality. Historians of science agree that Reinhold was not a closet Copernican.

Although Luther appears to have thought that Copernicus's cosmology conflicted with Scripture, he had advanced a hermeneutical principle that would allow Kepler, a "radical Copernican," to reconcile full heliocentrism with Scripture. This was the idea that Scripture often speaks in language of human appearances rather than in underlying and often counterintuitive laws of science. When Joshua 10 says the sun stood still, this may simply be the way the sun appeared to people, having no implications for the actual motion of the sun or earth.

The Broader Impact on Education

Christ's great commission (Matthew 28:19-20) enjoins his followers to make disciples and teach them everything he had commanded. Since Christ's teachings are written in a book, and only the educated can read and understand the message, fulfillment of the commission implies the need for universal education.

Luther realized that doctrinal corruption and abuses had occurred in part because so few people could access reliable Biblical information. Luther responded by translating the Bible into German (first printed in both testaments in 1534), and writing the *Small Catechism* in 1529. The printing press of Gutenberg for the first time made it possible to produce large quantities of books relatively quickly, leading to a wider distribution of more affordable copies.

---

17 Michael Hoskin and Owen Gingerich, "Medieval Latin Astronomy," in ed. Michael Hoskin, *The Cambridge Illustrated History of Astronomy* (Cambridge, UK: Cambridge University Press, 1997), 93.

Luther saw that there could be no reformation of the church without a reformation of education, that all Christians should be sufficiently educated to understand the Bible and Christian doctrine. Centuries ahead of his time, Luther called for a public school system, open to everyone, including primary and secondary schools, and universities.

The Lutheran founders of the scientific revolution were not enemies of Biblical Christianity, but faithful priests in the book of nature. The reformers did not censor learning, but encouraged everyone to discover the truths of Scripture and the knowledge and wisdom required to pursue vocations of service in the world. Indeed, Christian faith permeated all aspects of European life, including intellectual life.

ONGOING REFORMATION

With the death of young King Edward VI of tuberculosis in 1553, no males were left in the Tudor dynasty. Edward's sister became the queen.

Mary (1553-58)

Like her mother Catherine of Aragon, Mary Tudor was a Catholic, and during her brief reign she did what she could to reintroduce Catholicism. From the beginning, Mary made mistakes that were to alienate her from her own subjects, including her marriage to her cousin, Philip II the king of Spain, who would spend little time in England.

In her pro-Catholic program, the queen forced the clergy to give up their wives. She also had Latin reintroduced into worship. Most of the intellectual Protestant elite fled to the Continent; a few hundred people—about 300—were killed under "Bloody Mary." Among that number was Cranmer, who after wavering and recanting boldly confessed his faith and was burned at the stake in 1556. Nevertheless, Mary was unable to stem the Protestant tide.

Elizabeth (1558-1603)

Ascending to the throne on November 17, 1558, Anne's daughter, Elizabeth I, was to enjoy a long, glorious reign and become one of the most renowned sovereigns in history. The queen began her rule decisively, and by the end of 1558, Elizabeth's Act of Supremacy was in place.

While Elizabeth's religious convictions are not known for sure, she was most likely Protestant like her mother. She developed a moderate Protestant church, as she perceived it had been under her father. For Elizabeth, politics trumped theology, and the Church of England under the Elizabethan Settlement took the *via media*, the middle way. Elizabeth's

Act of Uniformity called for an inclusive version of the *Book of Common Prayer* (1559). The *Thirty-Nine Articles* (1562), also sought the middle way regarding sacraments and the doctrine of predestination. The 1559 *Book of Common Prayer* served not only the England of Elizabeth I and her Stuart successors, but it was the first Protestant prayer book used in America, brought by Jamestown settlers and others in the early 1600s.

In 1570, Pope Pius V excommunicated Elizabeth. Among those who took the injunction seriously was Elizabeth's erstwhile brother-in-law and suitor, Philip II of Spain. In 1588, this champion of the Counter Reformation assembled the "invincible" Armada, only to be defeated by the English fleet and Protestant winds.

Catholic and Lutheran Influences in *The Book of Common Prayer*

Even with publication of the *Book of Common Prayer* under Edward, the service retained Catholic elements, such as the commemoration of the Blessed Virgin and prayers for the dead. After years of Protestant teaching, one minister reported in 1559 that most of his parishioners still believed "that a man might be saved by his own weldoing" rather than through Christ.[18]

The Anglican Church is unique among Protestant churches in that it never broke with the basic organization of Catholicism. To this day, the Church of England retains the concept of apostolic succession, claiming its hierarchy traces back to the apostles by way of Roman Catholicism.

Thomas Cranmer, the single most influential figure in shaping Protestantism in England, was "Lutheran in his theology."[19] In compiling the *Book of Common Prayer,* Cranmer drew heavily from Lutheran catechisms and liturgies.

In 1540, Henry's chaplain Robert Barnes and secretary Thomas Cromwell were executed (for political more than theological reasons), thus dissipating much of the impact that Lutheranism might have had in England. Following Luther's death in 1546, Germans were less inclined to accept English refugees for fear of the Holy Roman Emperor Charles V. Lutheran influence lived on, as seen in the wording of the *Thirty-Nine Articles,* which reflect the Augsburg Confession in asserting, for instance, justification "by only faith in Jesus Christ."[20] Yet it was Calvinism that would predominate in English theology.

---
18   Luther D. Reed, *The Lutheran Liturgy* (Philadelphia: Fortress, 1947), 53. Many pastors would still say that today after centuries of Protestant teaching; Lutheran theology refers to the *opinio legis*—the religion of law, the idea of salvation by works—as the natural, innate religion of man, from which he only with difficulty emerges and into which he readily relapses.
19   Tim Dowley, ed., *Eerdman's Handbook to the History of Christianity* (Grand Rapids: Eerdmans, 1977), 390.
20   Dickens, *The English Reformation,* 252.

Arminian Humanism

Arminianism goes back to the Dutch theologian Jacobus Arminius (Jacob or James Harmensen, 1560-1609). His life spans the struggles of the Low Countries for independence from Spanish rule. The outcome of those struggles was that in 1607 three new countries were formed: Protestant Netherlands in the north, and Catholic Belgium and Luxemburg in the south.

Arminius had studied under John Calvin's successor Theodore Beza in Geneva. Centuries before the Reformation, Augustine had refuted the teachings of Pelagius, who had attributed to human beings the ability to work out their own salvation. Over the centuries, however, Roman theology had adopted a sort of semi-Pelagianism—crediting to God the initial infusion of grace, but leaving it to man to complete the project of salvation.

In his rediscovery of the Gospel, the good news of full and free salvation, Luther came to see salvation from beginning to end as entirely God's work, a free gift of grace. If, on the other hand, we are lost, it is our own doing, a rejection of God's grace. The Council of Trent (1546-63) anathematized this concept of the justification of sinners, pointing to human responsibility both in salvation and damnation. Calvin, and more particularly his followers, had developed a logically consistent schema. Emphasizing God's sovereignty, Calvinism came to see salvation and its opposite as entirely the work of God. This is the well-known double predestination dogma. God predestines some for salvation, others for damnation.

It was against this dogma, the "horrible decretum" of election, that Arminius took a stand. He argued that God predestined to salvation those who he foresaw would remain steadfast in the faith. This shifted the focus from God's sovereignty to something within man that merits salvation. It was a shift back toward the concept of salvation through works. Arminius was accused of Pelagianism, and the Synod of Dort posthumously condemned his teaching and developed the five points of strict Calvinism, with the appropriate English acronym TULIP:

T	total depravity	(of sinful human nature)
U	unconditional election	(without merit or achievement)
L	limited atonement	(Christ died only for the elect)
I	irresistible grace	(the elect are infallibly called)
P	perseverance of the saints	(those predestined can in no way fall away)

The debate continued long after the death of Arminius (his followers were called the Remonstrants), and it had profound effects in England. Arminianism came to represent such tendencies as liberalism, the propensity to attribute some sort of innate goodness to human nature, an emphasis on man's free will, an inclination toward an intellectualized interpretation of Scripture, and a leaning toward Rome.

The theological connections between England and the Netherlands were many. During and shortly after the reign of Elizabeth, in order to avoid Spanish persecution, an estimated 100,000 Dutch Protestants fled to England, accounting for five-sixths of all foreigners in England. Moreover, most people fleeing England were Calvinists. The Pilgrims came to America by way of the Netherlands. Today Jacob Arminius, the "grand old man of modernism," is little known. Nevertheless, his influence on English and Protestant theology has been vast.

Philosophical and Theological Issues

The Treaty of Westphalia not only ended the devastating Thirty Years' War (1618-48), but it also was to alter the spiritual climate of Europe. Wearied with war, the Continent began to see religious toleration as an option. In Germany, Calvinism now held equal footing with Catholicism and Lutheranism.

The seeds were sown for the acceptance of competing branches of Christianity—and much more. Two occurrences underscore this. The first was the development of Cartesian philosophy. According to a twentieth-century archbishop of Canterbury:

> [T]he most disastrous moment in European history occurred on that cold day in the winter of 1619-20 when the French philosopher Rene Descartes . . . concluded that there was only one thing he could not doubt—the fact that he doubted. From this he drew the celebrated conclusion *Cogito ergo sum*—"I think, therefore I am." . . . it was disastrous because it was a symptom of the dilemma of the modern mind. Doubt is put first. The individual self becomes the ultimate reference-point in thought.[21]

The other event was the acceptance of Arminianism in England. Among Arminian principles was the distinguishing of fundamental from nonfundamental doctrines. This fit with the Arminian tendency toward doctrinal flexibility. Theologian Otto Heick notes, "[I]t gradually made dogma second to ethics; it saw in Christ pre-eminently a new lawgiver, not the redeemer."[22] Arminianism especially protested against dogmas that conflicted with reason.

---

21 Dowley, *Eerdmans' Handbook to the History of Christianity*, 479.
22 Otto Heick, *A History of Christian Thought* (Philadelphia: Fortress, 1966), vol. 2, 81.

Yet the arts still rested on Christian foundations. Published in 1595, Philip Sidney's *An Apology [Defense] for Poetry*[23] was based on the Scriptures, and some of Sydney's poetry is simply setting psalms to English verse, as with Psalm 23:

> The lord the lord my shepherd is
>
> And so can never I
>
> Tast misery
>
> He rests me in green pasture his
>
> By waters still and sweet
>
> He guides my feet.[24]

. . . .

The Catholic Reformation

In response to the growing Protestant movement, the Roman Catholic Church convened a Council in Trent, Italy, between 1545 and 1563. The Council was a key part of the Catholic Reformation, also known as the Counter Reformation. Among the Council's decrees was the condemnation of the Protestant doctrine of justification through faith. The Catholic Reformation confirmed the Society of Jesus, the Jesuits, which had been founded by Ignatius Loyola (1491-1556); sought to restore the integrity of the papacy; and confirmed numerous Catholic doctrines, including purgatory and the invocation of saints. The Jesuit Order provided impetus to a revival of Catholicism and ushered in a massive wave of church and cathedral building.

Shakespeare and Donne

The age of Queen Elizabeth I was also the age of William Shakespeare (1564-1616), regarded as the greatest writer in English and the greatest dramatist in the world. His plays contain allusions to dozens of Biblical characters and fifty-five of the Bible's sixty-six books (some, such as Genesis and the Gospels, dozens of times).[25] Frequent references are made to Christ as Saviour, Redeemer, and Lord.[26] Woven into Shakespeare's work are numerous Christian themes, including "passages in *The Winter's Tale* (iv.3) and *The Tempest* (iv.1), where pre-marital intercourse is frowned upon, even between promised spouses. . . . a wise reminder of the true nature of human marriage, rooted in Christian tradition . . ."[27]

---

23   Philip Sidney, *An Apology for Poetry*, in Hazard Adams, ed., *Critical Theory since Plato* (Fort Worth: Harcourt, Brace, Jovanovich, 1992), 157.
24   Philip Sidney, *The Poems of Philip Sidney*, ed. William A. Ringer, Jr. (Oxford: Clarendon, 1962), 301.
25   See Richmond Noble, *Shakespeare's Biblical Knowledge and Use of the Book of Common Prayer* (London: Society for Prompting Christian Knowledge, 1935), 281-300.
26   William Burgess, *The Bible in Shakespeare* (Chicago and Winona Lake, IN: Winona, 1903), xii.
27   Peter Milward, *Shakespeare's Religious Background* (Chicago: Loyola, 1985), 229.

In Sonnet 146, Shakespeare deals with the ultimate issue—death and the resurrection, ending of the triumphant note of victory over death, through Christ ("thy servant"):

> . . . .
> Then soul, live thou upon thy servant's loss,
> And let that pine to aggravate thy store;
> Buy terms divine in selling hours of dross;
> Within be fed, without be rich no more:
> > So shalt thou feed on Death, that feeds on men,
> > And Death once dead, there's no more dying then.[28]

Like his contemporary Shakespeare, John Donne (1572-1631) was a child of his times, standing between the old Catholicism and the new Protestantism. Raised in the former, Donne finished his career as a clergyman in the latter. Much of his work is secular—such as the beautiful love poem "The Sun Rising." Moreover, much is explicitly spiritual. His most famous words are not from a poem but from a "Meditation": "No man is an island, entire of itself; every man is a piece of the continent, part of the main. . . . any man's death diminishes me, because I am involved in mankind, and therefore, never send to know for whom the bell tolls; it tolls for thee."[29] Prominent among the so-called "metaphysical" poets, confident of the life to come through Christ, Donne challenged death itself, as in the sonnet "Death Be Not proud":

> Death, be not proud, though some have called thee
> Mighty and dreadful, for, thou art not so,
> For, those whom thou thinkest thou dost overthrow,
> Die not, poor death, nor yet canst thou kill me;
> . . . .
> One short sleep past, we wake eternally,
> And death shall be no more, Death thou shalt die.[30]

Here Donne echoes St. Paul's words in 1 Corinthians 15—and quite possibly Shakespeare's in Sonnet 146. It was a time of faith—of men and women emboldened by the power of the Word.

---

28 William Shakespeare, *Shakespeare's Sonnets and Poems*, ed. Barbara A. Mowat and Paul Werstine (New York: Washington Square, 2006), 313.
29 John Donne, "XVII Meditation," *John Donne: The Major Works*, John Carey, ed. (Oxford and New York: Oxford University Press, 2000), 344.
30 Donne, "Death be not proud," *John Donne: The Major Works*, 175-6.

PART 2
THE AGE OF ENLIGHTENMENT: 1650—1800

THE RISE OF DEISM

The present is always a working out of the past. For seventeenth century England, this meant working through the issues of the religious Reformation and upheaval that had marked the previous century, when "almost all passion—intellectual, moral, personal, even political—was drawn into religious conflict."[31] Yet even amid the religious conflicts, Europeans shared much in common: "Even as they contended sometimes violently, Catholics and Protestants still agreed on the fundamentals of faith—the Trinity, the divinity of Christ, the authority of Scripture (however interpreted), miracles, the Ten Commandments, etc. . . . Unbelief seemed almost unthinkable."[32]

Given the political nature of the English Reformation, however, many in England felt that there had really been no real reformation in their country. Known as Puritans, they insisted on fundamental changes in doctrine and church organization. Puritans protested that the house of Stuart was ruling in an ungodly way; meanwhile the Parliament complained it was ruling in an unjust way. Civil war broke out; King Charles I was defeated and, in 1649, beheaded. For a dozen years, England was without a royal family, until the Restoration of the monarchy in 1660.

Despite the victory of the Puritans, who tended to be strict Calvinists, Arminianism had found a fertile field among English humanists and among certain eminent divines. Charles I had strong Arminian leanings and excluded Calvinist bishops from the royal counsels.

John Milton and *Paradise Lost*

John Milton (1608-74), a Puritan sympathizer, designed his epic poem *Paradise Lost,* 1667, to "justify the ways of God to man."[33] The

---
31 James Hitchcock, *What Is Secular Humanism?: Why Humanism Became Secular and How It Is Changing Our World* (Harrison, NY: RC Books, 1982), 31.
32 Hitchcock, *What Is Secular Humanism?*, 31.
33 John Milton, *Paradise Lost,* ed. Scott Elledge (New York: Norton, 1993), 9.

poem is grounded in Scripture and classical learning, as in the prologue he calls upon the Heavenly Muse, who for him is the Holy Spirit. His recounting of the Fall follows the Biblical account, with his own filling out of the story.

As with the Bible, Milton's epic ends in hope. Before expelling Adam and Eve from the garden, the "sovereign presence" spoke the first promise of the Savior who would be a descendant of Eve and come and crush the serpent's head (Genesis 3:15). Milton proceeds to identify that promise with its fulfillment in Jesus:

> Her seed shall bruise thy [the serpent's] head, thou shalt bruise his heel.
>
> So spake this oracle, then verified
>
> When Jesus son of Mary second Eve,
>
> Saw Satan fall like lightning down from heaven,
>
> Prince of the air; then rising from his grave
>
> Spoiled principalities and powers, triumphed
>
> In open show, and with ascension bright
>
> Captivity led captive through the air,
>
> The realm itself of Satan long usurped,
>
> Whom he shall tread at last under our feet.[34]

Though now living in a fallen creation, Eve expressed her confidence in that hope:

> This further consolation yet secure
>
> I carry hence; though all by me is lost,
>
> Such favour I unworthy am vouchsafed,
>
> By me the promised seed shall all restore.[35]

At the end of the epic, we see Adam and Eve leaving Eden:

> The world was all before them, where to choose
>
> Their place of rest, and providence their guide:
>
> They hand in hand with wandering steps and slow,
>
> Through Eden took their solitary way.[36]

The coming of Eve's "promised seed," awaited Milton's expounding in *Paradise Regained,* There, basing his work on the Gospel of Luke, the poet describes how Christ, the "Second Adam" resisted Satan's temptations and brought redemption. Milton regarded Biblical revelation as the source of true knowledge. At the same time, Milton's idea that he would "justify the ways of God to men" is rationalistic and reflects his Arminian leanings.

---

34 Milton, *Paradise Lost*, 234. See Luke 10:18; Ephesians 2:2; 4:8; 6:12.
35 Milton, *Paradise Lost*, 300.
36 Milton, *Paradise Lost*, 301.

Milton's published works echo Biblical truths, as evidenced in Sonnet 19, in which he dealt with the loss of his eyesight. This moving sonnet remains a great expression of Christian faith:

> When I consider how my light is spent,
>> Ere half my days, in this dark world and wide,
>> And that one talent which is death to hide
>> Lodged with me useless, though my soul more bent
> To serve therewith my Maker, and present
>> My true account, lest he returning chide,
>> "Doth God exact day-labor, light denied?"
> I fondly ask. But patience, to prevent
> That murmur, soon replies, "God doth not need
>> Either man's work or his own gifts; who best
>> Bear his mild yoke, they serve him best. His state
> Is kingly: thousands at his bidding speed,
>> And post o'er land and ocean without rest;
>> They also serve who only stand and wait."[37]

John Bunyan and *Pilgrim's Progress*

It is said that *Pilgrim's Progress from This World to That Which Is to Come* "has probably been more influential than any book other than the Bible."[38] *Pilgrim's Progress* by John Bunyan (1628-88) has been translated into more than 200 languages and has never been out of print. Like Bunyan's autobiography, *Grace Abounding to the Chief of Sinners,* it is an expression of deep and humble conviction. Lacking the immense scholarship and classical underpinnings of *Paradise Lost*, Bunyan's ingenious allegory is a classic in its own right. Steeped in the Bible and Christian teaching, at times the book's question and answer conversations seem to have been lifted straight from a catechism. Everything, including nature, attests to Scripture's teachings:

> MATTHEW. "Where have the clouds their water?"
> PRUDENCE. "Out of the sea."
> MAT. "What may we learn from that?"
> PRU. "That ministers should fetch their doctrine from God."
> MAT. "Why do they empty themselves upon the earth?"
> PRU. "To show that ministers should give out what they know
>> of God to the world."

---
37 Milton, Paradise Lost, 393.
38 Edward Albert, *A Short History of English Literature,* revised by G. G. Urwin (New York: Barnes and Noble, 1965), 64.

MAT. "Why is the rainbow caused by the sun?"

PRU. "To show that the covenant of God's grace is confirmed to us in Christ."[39]

The story of Christian's journey from the City of Destruction to the Celestial City is every man's story. It is the story of sin and grace, doubt and faith, destruction and salvation. From a literary standpoint, *Pilgrim's Progress* marks an early venture into an extended prose narrative. Written by a dissenting preacher who spent twelve years in prison for preaching without a license, it is perhaps the greatest literary monument of Protestantism. It is especially poignant that *Pilgrim's Progress* appeared even as the sun was beginning to set on the brief day of dissenting Protestantism in England.

In their *opera magna*, both Milton and Bunyan retained the old respect for Scripture. And while both stood in opposition to the establishment, they did not stand in opposition to basic Christian theology, including the central tenet of redemption through Christ.

Emmanuel Swedenborg

Other dissenting religionists, however, were not so closely tied to the Bible. A case in point was Emanuel Swedenborg (1688-1722), who was born in Sweden and spent the closing years of his life in England. Before turning to theology, he had established an international reputation as a polymath, having distinguished himself in numerous fields. In mid-life Swedenborg began to claim having religious visions and conversing with spirits and angels. Proclaiming himself a prophet and the herald of a new religion, Swedenborg moved away from the Lutheran doctrines he had been taught. For him the Trinity represented divine love, wisdom, and operation, which corresponded to the soul, body, and action in human beings. Swedenborg interpreted certain books of Scripture in a twofold sense—literal and spiritual—since he saw correspondences between nature and the spiritual world. After his death, Swedenborg's followers founded the New Church, also known as the Church of the New Jerusalem. The membership was never large, but, as will be seen, its significance would be.

The Spread of Secularism

In 1695, shortly after Milton and Bunyan had passed from the scene, England declared freedom of the press and put the country in the vanguard of the latest ideas. Already in 1690, John Locke had published *An Essay concerning Human Understanding* and *Treatise on Govern-*

---

39   John Bunyan, *The Pilgrim's Progress* (New York: Signet, 1964), 212.

ment, both works championing the individual mind. In *Reasonableness of Christianity*, 1695, Locke asserted that true faith cannot be contrary to reason; he denied the doctrines of human depravity and the atonement and set forth Jesus as the Law-giver and Teacher.[40]

At the end of the seventeenth century, such profound changes did not receive a great deal of attention from much of the population, or even from clerics: "In general, heterodox doctrines may have seemed less threatening to the security of orthodoxy at the time than they appear in retrospect."[41] Yet change was in the air. On the horizon loomed the movement known as deism.

English Deism: There Is a Supreme God

English deism goes back to Edward, Lord Herbert of Cherbury (ca. 1582-1648) and his *De Veritate* (1624). Edward Herbert represents the English-French interchange that was so much a part of the deistic movement. In his twenties, he made the first of many visits to France, where he came into contact with a culture that after a generation of religious war between Catholics and Protestants (1562-94) was saturated with "incredulity" where "irreligion was fashionable."[42]

Edward's concern with religious factionalism was a theme that was to run through deistic writings in general. Thomas Morgan (died 1743), for example, noted:

> The Jews would never admit of the Sense which the Christians have always put upon the Writings of Moses and the Prophets . . . But that is not all, for the Christians themselves could never agree about the Sense of their own Revelation, but have run into as many different and contrary Parties and Schemes upon it, as men of the most distant and opposite Religions of the World.[43]

For many, the solution to such strife lay in developing a rational concept of God, free from misunderstanding and argument. Rather than serving as a stepping-stone to revealed faith, this natural religion became an end in itself. Herbert held to a commonsense use of words and five "Common Notions" of religion: (1) "there is a Supreme God"; (2) "this Sovereign Deity ought to be Worshipped"; (3) the core of this worship is practice of virtue; (4) "vices and crimes . . . must be expiated by repentance"; (5) "there is a Reward or Punishment after this life."[44] God would not implant in people the desire for eternity unless he would fulfill it.

---

40   See L. Fuerbringer, Th. Engelder, and P. E. Kretzmann, *The Concordia Cyclopedia* (St. Louis: Concordia, 1927), 413.
41   W. M. Jacob, *Lay People and Religion in the Early Eighteenth Century* (Cambridge: Cambridge University Press, 1996), 111.
42   Eugene D. Hill, *Edward, Lord Herbert of Cherbury* (Boston: Twayne, 1987), 6.
43   Thomas Morgan, *The Moral Philosopher* (New York and London: Garland, 1977 [facsimile of 1737 edition]), 15-6.
44   Hill, *Edward, Lord Herbert of Cherbury*, 31.

In *An Essay concerning Human Understanding* (1690), John Locke expressed the same preference for natural religion over revelation:

> The volumes of interpreters, and commentators on the Old and New Testament, are but too manifest proofs of this [the imperfection of words]. Though everything said in the text is infallibly true, yet the reader may be, nay cannot choose but be very fallible in the understanding of it. . . . Since then the precepts of natural religion are plain and very intelligible to all mankind, and seldom come to be controverted; and other revealed truths, which are conveyed to us by books and languages, are liable to the common and natural obscurities and difficulties incident to words, methinks it would become us to be more careful and diligent in observing the former, and less magisterial, positive, and imperious in imposing our own sense and interpretations of the latter.[45]

According to Locke, the truths of revelation must commend themselves to human reason. Locke was but one of many to express such views. Among others were Anthony Ashley Cooper, Third Earl of Shaftesbury, "one of the chief proponents of natural religion."[46]

As deism progressed, it developed several strains. Some deists were concerned about rectifying what they saw as defects in the church. Others wanted to purify the religion at its foundation. Still others felt that revealed religion, especially Christianity, needed to go. "Nothing is so sad as the religious history of the eighteenth century," wrote a nineteenth century French critic, describing the religious climate of Europe in the age of Enlightenment. "In England and Germany a parching wind blows over hearts and minds. There is preached in the Protestant pulpits a religion without grandeur, without mysteries, which has neither the boldness of philosophy nor that of faith."[47]

English deism did not go unanswered by Biblical scholars. Foremost among the defenders of the faith was Joseph Butler, bishop of Durham (d. 1752), whose *The Analogy of Religion Natural and Revealed to the Constitution and Course of Nature* and other works are still published.[48] Heick calls *The Analogy* "the most complete and best answer given to the Deists' objections to a revealed religion," and he goes on to assert that "no opponent ventured to risk a reply."[49] In *The Analogy,* Butler points to the Bible's prophecies fulfilled and miracles, and argues:

> For though they may say, that the historical evidence of miracles, wrought in attestation of Christianity, is not sufficient to convince them that such miracles were really wrought, they cannot deny that there is such historical evidence, it being a known matter of fact

---

45 John Locke, *An Essay Concerning Human Understanding*, ed. Roger Woolhouse (London: Penguin, 1997), 436.
46 Norman L. Torrey, *Voltaire and the English Deists* (Archon Books, 1967), 104; Anthony Ashley Cooper, Third Earl of Shaftesbury, *Characteristics of Men, Manners, Opinions, Times*, ed. Lawrence E. Klein (Cambridge: Cambridge University Press, 1999).
47 Edmond de Pressensé quoted in William Forsyth, *The Novels and Novelists of the Eighteenth Century:* In *Illustration of the Manners and Morals of the Age* (New York: D. Appleton, 1871), 21.
48 See, for example, L. Rush Bush, ed. *Classical Readings in Christian Apologetics A. D. 100—1800* (Grand Rapids: Zondervan, 1983).
49 Heick, *A History of Christian Thought*, vol. 2, 110.

that there is. They may say, the conformity between the prophecies and events is by accident; but there are many instances in which the conformity itself cannot be denied.[50]

APOSTLES OF DEISM

Alexander Pope: The Proper Study of Mankind is Man

Alexander Pope (1688-1744) is the quintessential poet of the Augustan Age, so named as writers of the period sought to follow in the footsteps of the great Latin writers (e.g., Virgil) at the time of Caesar Augustus. In the style of his poetry Pope developed the heroic couplet to perfection, and in its content he spread the ideals of deism.

Raised a Roman Catholic in Protestant England, Pope knew what it meant to be a religious minority. The Catholics of Pope's day lived with it and carried on worship in the privacy of their homes. Such a background (and considering Pope's very name), however, was not sufficient to drive Pope away from the faith. Nor did it prevent him in his poetry from making favorable references to things Catholic, as when in *An Essay on Criticism,* he referred to St. Peter Cathedral in Rome:

> Thus when we view some well-proportion'd dome,
> (The world's just wonder, and ev'n thine, O Rome!)
> No single parts unequally surprise,
> All comes united to th' admiring eyes.[51]

An Essay on Man: Song of Enlightenment

In 1733, Pope published the initial epistles of *An Essay on Man*. Voltaire called it "the most beautiful, the most useful, and the most sublime didactic poem in any language,"[52] and one literary guide refers to it as "a compendium of popular Enlightenment ideas."[53] As we follow its outline, we will review some of the Enlightenment's key thoughts.

In the Prologue, Pope takes up Milton's defense of providence: "But vindicate the ways of God to Man." But unlike Milton's Biblically-based *Paradise Lost,* Pope's work is deistic.

The theme for the second section is that hope springs eternal. In the face of the unknown, death, and the ultimate, he urges, "Hope humbly then." Yet humility only goes so far, as we see the "proud Science" of the West set in vivid contrast to "the poor Indian" with "untutor'd mind."

---

50 Joseph Butler, *The Analogy of Religion,* in Bush, *Classical Readings in Christian Apologetics,* 344-5.
51 Alexander Pope, *Pope: Poems,* selected by Douglas Grant (London and New York: Penguin Books, 1985), 21. Subsequent references to Pope's work are from this edition.
52 As quoted in Will and Ariel Durant, *The Age of Voltaire,* vol. 9 in *The Story of Civilization* (New York: Simon and Schuster, 1965), 175.
53 Marion Wynne-Davis, *Prentice Hall Guide to English Literature* (New York: Prentice Hall, 1990), 497.

In the third section, we come to the famous clarion call for the age of reason:

> Know then thyself, presume not God to scan,
> The proper study of mankind is Man.

Reason must be on its guard, for "What Reason weaves, by Passion is undone." Pope depicts man as hovering between God and the Beast.

Next, Pope points to the wisdom of God above all human limitations: "Tho' Man's a fool, yet God IS WISE." While human beings may foolishly build castles in the air, God is in the heavens, and "Behind the scenes, all is well." For positive thinking deists, such as Pope, God the great Watchmaker, though unseen, has created the best of all worlds.

Fifthly, another Enlightenment theme is that of happiness, "our being's end and aim!" The theme of the pursuit of happiness brings to mind thoughts of the birth of the United States with its ideal of the inalienable rights of "life, liberty, and the pursuit of happiness."

In the sixth part, "Calm Sunshine or Fame" is the theme. For deists, right actions were much more important than doctrines. Pope expressed this with his: "Act well your part, there all the honour lies." As he had put it earlier in the poem:

> On faith and hope the world will disagree,
> But all mankind's concern is charity.

In the Epilogue, Pope summarizes much of what represents the Enlightenment and its influence through the years:

> For Wit's false mirror held up Nature's light;
> Show'd erring Pride, "WHATEVER IS, IS RIGHT;"
> That Reason, Passion, answer one great aim;
> That true SELF-LOVE and SOCIAL are the same;
> That VIRTUE only makes our Bliss below;
> And all our knowledge is, OURSELVES TO KNOW.

"WHATEVER IS, IS RIGHT" is a theme that runs throughout the *Essay*. The shift from Milton's *Paradise Lost* to Pope's *An Essay on Man* marks a transition toward an anthropocentric worldview. *An Essay on Man* epitomizes the Enlightenment values of deism, humanism, reason, and the moral life. Yet it recognizes the power of passion, both as a positive and negative force. In this, Pope shows the limitations of reason and prefigures Romanticism.

The Dying Christian to His Soul

Along with what we might call the humanistic-deistic element in the poet, there was another side to Pope. Among Pope's works is a short poem, "The Dying Christian to His Soul." Written in 1736 and later set to music, this piece exudes a spirit of hope grounded in Christian faith:

> The world recedes; it disappears!
> Heav'n opens on my eyes! my ears
> With sounds seraphic ring:
> Lend, lend your wings! I mount! I fly!
> O Grave! where is thy Victory?
> O Death! where is thy Sting?

Pope describes the Christian's passage into immortality. The poem's closing lines are taken from the Bible (1 Corinthians 15). Although Pope was a deist, he held to tenets of Christianity, an inconsistency not uncommon in human nature and essential in British pragmatism.

Voltaire: *Ecrasez l'infâme!*

Voltaire (1694-1778) was six years Pope's junior and would outlive him by thirty-four years. Their relationship shows the cosmopolitan world of the eighteenth century Enlightenment as well as the contrast between mild and virulent strains of deism. Born Francois-Marie Arouet, Voltaire would become the most famous of the *philosophes* and perhaps the most noted skeptic of all time. It is of interest that while Pope lived as a Catholic in Protestant England, Voltaire, who lived and died a Catholic in Catholic France, became much more skeptical and anti-religious.

Typical for men of letters, religion was an all-consuming passion for Voltaire: "[I]n the eighteenth century religion and philosophy [which terms, Voltaire used 'almost interchangeably'] were still considered to be important subjects for intellectual discourse . . . A statistical survey of the more than twenty thousand letters in the corpus of the correspondence reveals that at least half of them contains either direct or tangible references to philosophy in the secondary [religious] sense of the term."[54] Voltaire was preoccupied with ultimate questions.

Voltaire and the English Deists

Voltaire's intimate connections with English deism are not surprising: "[T]he intellectual ties between England and France were close, the prestige of English philosophers was high. The fashion of deism was a daughter of Anglomania."[55] Between 1726 and 1729, Voltaire lived in England, where he learned English. When he arrived, he was "already considerable steeped in Deism, in the new scientific thought, and the

---
[54] Arnold Ages, "Voltaire and the Problem of Atheism: The Testimony of the Correspondence," Neophilologus. 68:4 (October 1984): 504.
[55] Peter Gay, *The Enlightenment An Interpretation: The Rise of Modern Paganism* (New York and London: W. W Norton, 1977), 382.

conviction that there should be no restraint on the individual's right to examine objectively and to express himself on all human institutions and thought, including government and religion."[56]

While in England, Voltaire became acquainted with Pope. According to Oliver Goldsmith, the meeting of the two men was to leave a lasting impression on Voltaire:

> When [Voltaire] first entered the room, and perceived our poor melancholy English poet, naturally deformed, and wasted as he was with sickness and study, he could not help regarding him with the utmost compassion. But, when Mr. Pope began to speak, and to reason upon moral obligations, and dress the utmost delicate sentiments in the most charming diction, Voltaire's pity began to be changed into admiration and . . . envy.[57]

Yet for all his admiration of Mr. Pope, Voltaire was his own man. More philosophical than Pope and less satisfied with accepting things as they were, Voltaire was not content with Pope's mild form of deism. He would take up a virulent deism that led to vehement attacks on religion.

Voltaire returned to France. Impressed with the English, he had composed a series of letters praising English freedom. Despite his efforts to keep them from publication in France, the letters appeared in 1734. Voltaire fled to exile and took up residence with Mme. du Chatelet on her estate at Cirey, beyond the reach of the king of France.

Candide and *Reflections on Religion*

For Voltaire, the Lisbon earthquake of 1756 undermined any sort of optimistic philosophy. Perhaps his exile and the death of Mme. du Chatelet in 1749 added to the sense of gloom. Voltaire's hostility to optimism is evident in his most famous work *Candide* (1759). Here he lampoons the German philosopher Leibniz (1646-1716) and his theodicy. Leibniz becomes the ever upbeat, but laughable tutor Pangloss who constantly wants to talk philosophically about "the best of all possible worlds . . . and pre-established harmony."[58]

At book's end, Candide responds with the book's closing line, "That is well put, but we must cultivate our garden" (100). Ultimately, Voltaire offers the same advice as Pope: Look to yourself and do the best you can in your little sphere of influence. But behind that advice lies none of the optimism that all is well.

During Voltaire's Cirey period, he and Mme. du Chatelet spent time researching and together formed their opinions on what were to become their religious polemics. After her death, Voltaire's life-mission was

---
56 Kenneth W. Appelgate, trans., *Voltaire on Religion: Selected Writings* (New York: Frederick Unger, 1974), 3-4.
57 As quoted in Maynard Mack, *Alexander Pope: A Life* (New York: W. W. Norton, 1985), 447.
58 Voltaire, *Candide and Other Stories* trans. Roger Pearson (Oxford and New York: Oxford University Press, 1998), 97-8. The subsequent references to *Candide* are from this edition

twofold: *écrasez l'infâme* (crush the infamy [of ignorance, superstition, and fanaticism]) and improve French society. In introducing Voltaire's polemics, translator Kenneth Appelgate notes: "Commentators have remarked [on] his numerous errors and inaccuracies, . . . Their significance in estimating the worth and reliability of Voltaire's arguments and conclusions will necessarily be an individual decision."[59]

What follows is a representative sampling of Voltaire's polemics. We leave it to readers to note Voltaire's "errors and inaccuracies."

> The innumerable faults in geography and chronology and the contradictions that are found in the Pentateuch have forced many Jews and Christians to maintain that it could not be the work of Moses.[60]

In the New Testament, Voltaire criticizes the Gospel accounts of Jesus' life and Jesus himself:

> Pray tell me, when you go to a wedding party, how God, who also went to the wedding party, changed water into wine for people who were already drunk?
>
> Shall I say with Luke that Jesus ascended into heaven from the small village of Bethany? Shall I insinuate, with Matthew, that this happened in Galilee where the disciples saw him for the last time? (34-5)

Voltaire ranges through the Bible and into church history, pointing out whatever he sees as contradictions, foolishness, wickedness, and problems of every kind. He finishes:

> I conclude that all sensible men, all honest men must hold the Christian religion in dread. "The great name of Theist, that is not revered enough" [quotation from Shaftesbury's *Characteristics*] is the sole name that we should take. The only Gospel that we ought to read is the great book of nature, written by the hand of God and sealed with his seal. The only religion that we ought to profess is to *adore God and be an honest man*. (212)

Considering that in the century after Voltaire's death, Christianity expanded around the world as never before, his assault on the Bible was not successful. Given his vehement attacks on religion, it is often assumed that he was an atheist, in the strict sense of the word, one who believes there is no God. Throughout his life he remained a deist and took issue with atheism.[61] In spite of his attacks upon the church, Voltaire died a natural death and still a Catholic.

The Legacy of Deism

The roots of deism were in English soil, but it would be transplanted and flourish on the Continent, especially in France. Much is made of the

---
59   Appelgate, *Voltaire on Religion*, 16.
60   As quoted in Appelgate, 97-8. Subsequent quotations are from this volume.
61   Cf. Ages, "Voltaire and the Problem of Atheism."

deism of some of the Founding Fathers of the United States. For the most part, those statesmen were confessing Christians.[62] Today most of the deists are not read. Theologian Ernst Troeltsch (d. 1925) characterized them as "second- and third-rate men who had the real intelligentsia of England against them."[63] Yet they played a part in the Enlightenment—the Age of Reason. While most of the deists are forgotten, the names of Alexander Pope and Voltaire live on. They were truly apostles of deism.

THE TROUBLED EIGHTEENTH CENTURY

Like its counterparts in France and Germany, English Deism was not a religiously neutral force but became evermore hostile to Christian faith. In response to increasing attacks on faith, Christians appealed to the argument from design to affirm God's existence and defended the Bible by showing its authors were reliable. And although faith was becoming less sharply focused, it remained strong and for most everyone, God was still central to life.

Latitudinarianism

By the 1700s, the Dissenters—those who disagreed with the Church of England—had lost most of their support among the nobility and gentry who mattered in politics, and the state church was dominated by "men of latitude." The famous preacher John Tillotson (d. 1694), archbishop of Canterbury, had been among their number, as was the Earl of Shaftesbury, whose approach to ethics rested on an optimistic view of innate human goodness, a view removed from the Christian doctrines of the Fall and original sin.

Practical religion was the aim of Latitudinarians. Bishop Burnet, himself one of them, spoke highly of their "simplicity" and how their preaching "was clear, plain, and short."[64] Although the Latitudinarians included many devout clergy, low-temperature spirituality became the order of the day by the early eighteenth century. Lukewarm church men swelled the Anglican ranks:

> The church of England not only failed to offer the most rudimentary services to thousands of the poor, but its doctrines and services increasingly failed to inspire the educated and the wealthy. Upper-class Anglicans in the first half of the eighteenth century wanted . . . morality taught, not theology. Tired of the furious doctrinal disputes of the seventeenth century, they wished their parsons to avoid the dogmatic, mystical, and emotional. To worship the supreme being, repeat the creeds, and lead a moral life was

---

62 See John Eidsmoe, *Christianity and the Constitution: The Faith of Our Founding Fathers* (Grand Rapids, MI: Baker, 1995).
63 Heick, *A History of Christian Thought*, vol. 2, 108.
64 Heick, *A History of Christian Thought*, vol. 2, 91.

sufficient. . . . This outlook, called Latitudinarianism, became dominant among eighteenth-century bishops, the lower clergy, and the governing classes.[65]

But the Latitudinarian movement, like its counterparts on the Continent, "soon lost itself in indifferentism and thus became unproductive in theology."[66] There were some 13,500 clerics in England, and against many of them the laity harbored resentment for their pretensions "to wisdom or to riches. . . ." This anticlericalism did "not necessarily imply antipathy towards the Christian faith"; and, in fact, "there is strong evidence that the Christian religion, and the Church of England in particular, were in good heart during most of the first half of the eighteenth century."[67] Nevertheless, a growing religious indifference was in evidence.

The Methodist Revival

Amid the lukewarm reasonableness of Latitudinarian England came the Methodist revival. At the center of this revival were George Whitefield, Charles Wesley, and, most prominently, his brother John. In 1748, when John Wesley was thirty-four years old, he had an experience in London that would change his life. He described it in his journal:

> In the evening I went very unwillingly to a society in Aldersgate Street, where one was reading Luther's preface to the Epistle to the Romans. . . . while the leader was describing the change which God works in the heart through faith in Christ, I felt my heart strangely warmed. I felt I did trust in Christ alone for salvation; and an assurance was given me that He had taken away my sins, even mine, and saved me from the law of sin and death.[68]

From that point on, he was on fire for preaching. By the time he died in 1791, Wesley had preached some 40,000 sermons, many of them in the open air to thousands, and traveled a quarter of a million miles, mostly on horseback and while reading.

Yet Wesley, the founder of Methodism, himself was influenced by Arminianism, as seen in his emphasis on the freedom of the will and on ethics over doctrine.[69] Wesley attacked the Gospel preaching he saw as a "harangue on the sufferings of Christ or salvation without strongly inculcating holiness."[70] Wesley's parents were Arminians; his mother wrote to him that the Calvinist doctrine of God's predestinating some to hell was shocking. Wesley had the letter printed in the first issue of *The Arminian Magazine*.

---

65 Clayton Roberts, and David Roberts. *A History of England*, vol. 2, *1688 to the Present*. Englewood Cliffs, NJ: Prentice-Hall, 1985), 456.
66 Heick, *A History of Christian Thought*, vol. 2, 91.
67 Jacob, *Lay People and Religion in the Early Eighteenth Century*, 44.
68 Quoted in Aldersgate United Methodist Church (Wheaton, IL) website. http://www.gbgm-umc.org/aldersgate-wheaton/aumcname.html
69 Cf. James Downey, *The Eighteenth Century Pulpit: A Study of the Sermons of Butler, Berkeley, Secker, Sterne, Whitefield and Wesely* (Oxford: Clarendon Press, 1969), 200.
70 Downey, *The Eighteenth Century Pulpit*, 207.

The Methodist Revival in England came on the heels of the First Great Awakening in the American colonies, which was spearheaded by preachers such as Jonathan Edwards (1703-58) and the Anglican George Whitefield (1714-70), who was able deeply to move Benjamin Franklin, if not convert him. Franklin became a lifelong friend of Whitefield.

The Birth of the English Novel

Along with spiritual revival, England was experiencing a growing middle class. With more money, the ability to read, and more free time, people were ready for the newest form of information and entertainment—the extended narrative, the novel. Daniel Defoe was one of the first novelists, whose *Robinson Crusoe*, 1719, reflected the temperament of the times: "secularizing shift in Calvinism, which was taking place."[71]

Published three years after *Robinson Crusoe,* Defoe's *Moll Flanders* tells the story of the female counterpart of Robinson Crusoe. Set adrift in society, she must find her way. As a young woman, she relies on her beauty. Later, she turns to stealing for a living. In the end, she finds economic and marital stability in America, but not until she has come to spiritual terms with life. In prison and sentenced to die, Moll meets a minister who explains to her "the Terms of Divine Mercy, which according to him consisted of nothing more, or more Difficult than that of being sincerely desirous of it, and willing to accept it."[72] The minister also brings Moll a reprieve. While she does not revert to a criminal life, her materialistic interests quickly return.

Jonathan Swift's *Gulliver's Travels,* 1726-7, satirizes the foibles of society. Swift, a clergyman, may have been more in tune with the academic-intellectual currents of the day than the journalist Defoe. Swift's Gulliver takes up the issue of reason. Gulliver's final preference for the company of horses over human beings, including his own family, underscores the barrenness of reason without emotion. Swift clearly shared the Biblical view of human nature as fallen. But he does not rise to anything approaching Bunyan's triumphant grace abounding.

Samuel Richardson's epistolary novel *Clarissa,* 1747-8, reflects the times: "in Richardson's time religion had become largely a matter of ethics rather than dogma."[73] Having been raped by the villain Lovelace, Clarissa becomes ill and dies. In words reminiscent of *Pilgrim's Progress,* while dying, she looks toward the heavenly city and says, "I am entering upon a better tour than to France or Italy either!"[74] For Lovelace,

---

71   Erich Kahler, *The Inward Turn of Narrative*, translated by Richard and Clara Winston (Evanston, IL: Northwestern University Press, 1973), 95.
72   Daniel Defoe, *Moll Flanders* (Oxford and New York: Oxford University Press, 1971), 289.
73   Leopold Damrosch, Jr., *God's Plot & Man's Stories: Studies in the Fictional Imagination from Milton to Fielding* (Chicago and London: University of Chicago Press, 1985), 262.
74   Samuel Richardson, *Clarissa*, ed. George Sherburn (Boston: Houghton Mifflin, 1962), 462. Subsequent references to page numbers are in included the text.

too, death is the way out. Richardson says that although "he seemed very unwilling to die," his last words were, "LET THIS EXPIATE!" (516) As he died, he "refused . . . the Sacraments in the Catholic way" (516). This was not from any Protestant conviction. Rather, Lovelace saw his own death as payment for his wrongs toward Clarissa. Neither Clarissa's nor Lovelace's death expresses faith in Christ as the Savior; they themselves are seen as a payment for guilt. *Clarissa* is a couple of generations removed from *Paradise Lost* and *Pilgrim's Progress,* and like so much literature of the time, it illustrates how religion was shifting from a specific, Biblical content toward a generalized system of morality.

Henry Fielding's novel *Tom Jones,* 1749, also underscores this. Throughout his life as a public servant, Fielding was involved in social causes such as criminal and postal reform. Like Bunyan's Christian, Fielding's Tom Jones is everyman. Moreover, Tom's journey from the country to the city and finally to a happy ending back in the country parallels the theme of paradise lost and the journey to heaven—paradise regained. But the concerns have changed; his narrative focuses on earthly ends. Since Fielding's main concern is with hypocrisy, he winks at Tom's sexual escapades. The problem for Tom is not his immorality, but his naiveté. Tom needs to see his actions in the context of their consequences. In other words, he needs to apply reason.

As *Pilgrim's Progress* was the culmination of Dissenter literature, *Tom Jones* was the literary epitome of the Age of Reason. While Tom Jones was frolicking through the English countryside, on the Continent Jean-Jacques Rousseau (1712-78) was arguing, "Neither the laws nor the government of a state are appointed by God. They are based on the general will of the people,"[75] and Voltaire was advocating the end of Christianity.

Aesthetics

It is noteworthy that at this time Alexander Gottlieb Baumgarten coined the term "aesthetics" in his *Reflections on Poetry* (1735) and his unfinished *Aesthetica* (1750, 1758).[76] He felt that philosophy needed to be rounded off with the addition of a study of the "inferior cognition," namely, that of the senses.[77] "*Aesthetica,*" wrote Baumgarten, "*est scientia cognitionis sensitivae*" (Aesthetics is the science of sensory knowing).[78] Art was taking on a life of its own, apart from its spiritual moorings.

---

75   Dowley, *Eerdmans' Handbook to the History of Christianity,* 492.
76   Monroe C. Beardsley, *Aesthetics from Classical Greece to the Present: A Short History* (University, AL: University of Alabama Press, 1976), 156.
77   Harold Osborne, ed., *Aesthetics in the Modern World* (New York: Weybright and Talley, 1968), 15.
78   Alexander Gottlieb Baumgarten, *Aesthetica.* (Hildesheim: Georg Olms Verlagsbuchhandlung, 1961), 1.

Troubled Times

Even as reason was being extolled, it was being called into question. Skepticism in Britain began with David Hume, who came to question everything. In his treatise *Of the Standard of Taste*, 1757, Hume concluded that there is more agreement in questions of artistic taste than of reason: "The same Homer, who pleased at Athens and Rome two thousand years ago, is still admired in Paris and London...." Moral principles, abstract philosophy, religious systems, and speculative opinions, however, "are in a continual flux and revolution."[79]

In August 1776 the writer James Boswell met with the dying Hume. Boswell had "hoped to find Hume reconciled to the Christian religion, only to discover that he was stoically resigned to the prospect of everlasting annihilation. This deeply affected Boswell, who had an intense fear of death and whose hold on religion was none too secure."[80] Indeed, Boswell's life was a wild mix of religion, literary discussions with the likes of Dr. Johnson, and sexual promiscuity, "... caused by his rejection of the strict Calvinist upbringing of his youth and his rapid passage through Methodism and Catholicism into skepticism and then to a somewhat lukewarm Anglican Episcopalianism."[81] *Boswell's London Journals, 1762-1763* capture Boswell's ambivalence: "SUNDAY 16 JANUARY. I heard service and sermon in the New Church in the Strand ... I then went to Louisa [his mistress] and was permitted the rites of love with great complacency."[82] It seems most people did not share Hume's stoic resignation but, like Boswell, struggled.

The novel *Tristram Shandy*, 1759-67, is as interesting for its author, Laurence Sterne, as for the story itself.[83] Sterne was a pastor, who published sermons as well as his unconventional novel. Known to some as a philanderer and dilatory in his pastoral functions, his book brought him fame and success. Typical of Latitudinarian clergy, Sterne had "only a peripheral interest" in doctrine, and the purpose of religion, said Sterne, "is to purify our hearts ... in a word, to make us wiser and better men—better neighbours—better citizens—and better servants to God."[84] By the end of *Tristram Shandy*, the old soldier Toby has taken center stage, involved in a comedy of misunderstandings with Widow Wadman. She wants to find out where he was wounded—she being interested in what part of his body—and he thinks of what particular battlefield.

---

79   Hume, *Of the Standard of Taste*, in Adams, *Critical Theory since Plato*, 310.
80   Lawrence Stone, *The Family, Sex and Marriage: In England 1500-1800* (New York: Harper Torchbooks, 1979), 367.
81   Stone, *The Family, Sex and Marriage: In England 1500-1800*, 374-5.
82   James Boswell. *Boswell's London Journal 1762-1763*, ed. Frederick A. Pottle (New Haven and London: Yale University Press, 1950), 144-5.
83   Laurence Sterne, *Tristam Shandy*, ed. Howard Anderson (New York and London: W. W. Norton, 1980).
84   Downey, *The Eighteenth Century Pulpit*, 129.

For Great Britain the eighteenth century was a period of profound change. By 1760, Britain was on the verge of an agricultural revolution and population explosion. Between 1760 and 1820, the population mushroomed from 6.5 to 12 million, while, because of improved agricultural efficiency, the food supply increased accordingly.[85] Following the Seven Years' War (1756-63), Great Britain ruled the seas and was on its way to becoming the greatest power in the world—in spite of the loss of the American Revolution.

As historic Christianity assumed an increasingly peripheral role for many, other concerns pressed toward the center. Yet the old dictum of Augustine that the human heart is restless till it rests in God holds true amid even the strongest onslaughts of rationalism and skepticism. Living during the turbulent Age of Reason, Sir Isaac Watts (1674-1748)—the "father of English hymnody"—found his anchor in the God of Scripture, as expressed in one of his many hymns:

> O God, our help in ages past,
>
> Our hope for years to come,
>
> Our shelter from the stormy blast,
>
> And our eternal home.[86]

WOMEN WRITERS

Although the eighteenth century typically brings to mind thoughts of the Age of Enlightenment or Age of Reason, it does not lend itself to simple classification. The first half of the century took up where the previous century had ended, as religious wars gave way to international power struggles. In mid century, the Seven Years' War pitted Prussia, Hanover, and England against Austria, Russia, Saxony, Spain, Sweden, and France. From this international conflict—in a sense, the first world war—England outstripped France for global supremacy. The end of the century witnessed the great revolutions in America and France.

Writers were a part of these changes. The novel became the prevailing type of English literature, and most of those novels were written by women, as was much poetry. Prominent among early women writers was Charlotte Lennox whose *The Female Quixote*, 1752, deals with women in society. Raised in a remote English castle, the heroine Arabella develops her view of reality by reading poorly translated French romances. After numerous misadventures and misunderstandings, often of a humorous nature, she finally gets things straight and marries. Helping straighten her out was "the good Divine," who leads her to distinguish fact from fiction in literature. This "Miracle" of reason enables Arabella to get on with her life.

---
85 Roberts and Roberts, *A History of England*, vol. 2, 456.
86 Isaac Watts, "O God, Our Help in Ages Past," hymn 441 in *Christian Worship*.

Sarah Scott's *Millenium Hall*

In 1762, Sarah Robinson Scott (1723-95) published *A Description of Millenium Hall*.[87] Although not widely recognized, the novel shows the growing role of women and expresses eighteenth century spirituality. *Millenium Hall* is one long—200 pages!—epistolary novel depicting life in eighteenth century England, especially the life of women.

Millenium Hall and Bluestocking Feminism

Millenium Hall is told from a male point of view, but it reflects "bluestocking' feminism." The term bluestocking comes from the custom of middle class women wearing blue rather than the traditional black stockings. This was an early expression of feminism and symbolized the admission of women into the trading and merchant classes.

Later in the century, inspired by the American and French Revolutions, English feminists became more radical. Most notable among them was Mary Wollstonecraft, whose *Vindication of the Rights of Woman* (1792) has become a benchmark of world feminism. There is nothing subtle about Wollstonecraft's appeal: "Would men but generously snap our chains, and be content with rational fellowship instead of slavish obedience, they would find us more observant daughters, more affectionate sisters, more faithful wives, more reasonable mothers—in a word, better citizens."[88] Writing three decades after Scott, Wollstonecraft speaks of feminism as a tool toward making better *citizens*. For Scott, the goal is making better *Christians* and members of humanity.

Millenium Hall and Christian Faith

According to the book of Revelation, chapter 20, Satan will be bound for 1000 years (Greek *chilias*, Latin *millennium*), during which Christ and his people will reign. This is symbolic language referring to the New Testament period when the Gospel will prosper and Satan will be held in check. After that, Satan will have free rein for a brief time before the end. Some, however, understand this as a literal 1000-year period with a literal paradise on earth for that time. Scott follows this interpretation. It came out of a period when many Dissenters looked for the establishment of a New Jerusalem in England. She may have used the term "millenium" (as she spells it, with one n) figuratively, but she clearly applied it to situations in the England of her day. The story takes place in Cornwall (56), where Camelot was.

---

[87] Sarah Scott, *A Description of Millenium Hall*, Gary Kelly, ed. (Peterborough, Ontario, 1995), 56. Subsequent quotations from the novel are from this edition and pages numbers are noted in parentheses in the text.
[88] Mary Wollstonecraft, *Vindication of the Rights of Woman*, in *The Portable Enlightenment Reader*, ed. Isaac Kramnick (New York: Penguin, 1995), 628.

Separated from her husband not long after they were married, Scott joined with a friend to organize programs for needy women. In one such program, they taught poor girls how to make bed linens and clothes. In addition to assisting them in physical matters, on Sunday mornings, Scott instructed the young women in the catechism and saw to it that they went to church. Scott sets forth in *Millenium Hall* a Christianity reduced to the lowest common denominator of leading a good life. In *Millenium Hall,* the Bible is valuable because it is the repository of "the Christian's law" (166), not because it makes people "wise for salvation through faith in Christ Jesus" (2 Timothy 3:15). Heaven is mentioned (79), but only as a reflection of earthly innocence.

The Christianity espoused in *Millenium Hall* is a religion of social change and one that focuses on the enhancement of this world. When the "reason and piety" (242) of the women of Millenium Hall emanate out into society and the world, everyone will be the better for it.

Charlotte Smith's *Desmond*

"Bliss was it in that dawn to be alive, but to be young was very heaven." These words of William Wordsworth summarized the feelings of many in England and throughout Europe during the early, heady days of the French Revolution. For many, *this* was the millennium, less the fulfillment of religious hope than the outcome of political action.

In 1792, during the optimistic period of the Revolution, Charlotte Smith (1749-1806) published *Desmond*, thirty years after Scott's *Millenium Hall.* Much had changed during that time. The spinning machine and steam engine had been developed—inventions that helped establish Britain as the world's first industrial nation—and the revolutions in America and France would forever alter political thought. Meanwhile, cultural and literary changes involved an increasing emphasis on emotions. This was the "cult of sensibility," with feelings as the highest realization of what it meant to be human. The much-revered Jane Austen (1775-1817) read Smith's novels and responded to them in her works, including *Sense and Sensibility.*

Desmond and Romantic Fiction

In a marriage she described as "worse than African bondage,"[89] to a husband who spent time in debtor's prison and was given to drinking, adultery, and violence, Charlotte Smith had to provide for their twelve children. She turned to writing novels. Smith's *Desmond* is the only one of her eleven novels for which she enlisted the epistolary form, a form

---

89 Charlotte Smith, *Desmond*, ed. Antje Blank and Janet Todd (Peterborough, Ontario: Broadview, 2001), 7. Subsequent quotations from the novel are from this edition and pages numbers are noted in parentheses in the text.

that was on its way out. As romantic fiction, *Desmond* is the story of the love between Desmond and Geraldine, yet true to the eighteenth-century *Zeitgeist*, Smith also extols reason. But reason is overshadowed by the story's emphasis on sensibility, here seen in its most noble expression, longing for the welfare of others. Smith was an important literary link to the nascent Romantic Movement.

Desmond and the French Revolution

The French Revolution had not yet slid into the bloody Reign of Terror, and Smith saw in France a model for England. Not everyone shared that optimism. Prominent among those who reacted negatively was Edmund Burke. In Burke's *Reflections on the French Revolution* (1790), he criticized the French Revolution for wandering from the principles of true liberty and, at the same time, extolled the virtues of the British government and people: "we have not neglected religion."[90] Burke was supported by others, such as the notable Evangelical Hannah More (1745-1833), who took issue with the religious radicalism of the pro-revolutionists, the Jacobins.

Two thirds of Smith's novel relates to a discussion of the French Revolution. She had gained her knowledge of France partly through personal experience, when in order to escape creditors she and her husband had spent some time living in Normandy from 1784 to 1785. The France she depicts is diametrically opposed to that of Burke. Parallel to her treatment of what was going on in France, Smith weaves another theme, namely, the need for freedom and equality for women. The widespread awareness of feminist issues as evidenced in Wollstonecraft's *Rights of Women*, also published in 1792, was a factor, along with Smith's marriage to a ne'er-do-well.

Desmond and Religion

The novel *Desmond* endorses Voltaire, and Smith does not have Geraldine, a woman in despair, talk about the hope and strength that can come from a Christian faith. Watching a procession of priests, that unbeknown to her includes Desmond in disguise, Geraldine observes, "All religion . . . is not abolished in France" (325). Yet throughout the novel, there is little mention of religion. During the course of her writing career, Smith became friends with several notable literary figures, including William Cowper (1731-1800), who wrote hymns such as "God Moves in a Mysterious Way" and "There Is a Fountain Filled with Blood":

> There is a fountain filled with blood
>
> Drawn from Immanuel's veins,

---

90 Edmund Burke, *The Portable Edmund Burke*, ed. Isaac Kramnick (New York: Penguin, 1999), 461-2.

>And sinners plunged beneath that flood
>Lose all their guilty stains.[91]

In *Desmond* religion works more as a prop for the display of emotions than as their source.

Toward the end of the novel, the character Verney, having been wounded in a fight, has a deathbed conversion of sorts. He asks "forgiveness for all the injuries he had done to [his family] and to [Geraldine]" (369). This is a moving scene, not because the gates of heaven are opened to a sinner, but because it shows that people can change. The story closes with Desmond contemplating the likelihood that Geraldine will be his wife. "Heaven grant it!" he exclaims (414). This is about as close as he comes to prayer. Half a century removed from the heyday of deism, such references to the deity show a personal, emotional aspect of faith missing in deism. Yet they are equally removed from a personal faith in the triune God and historic Christianity.

Ann Radcliffe and the Gothic Novel

The preeminent author of Gothic fiction was Ann Radcliffe (1764-1823). Published in 1791, at the time of the French Revolution—midway between the storming of the Bastille (1789) and the symbolic enthronement of reason in the Cathedral of Notre Dame and execution of Louis XVI (1793)—Radcliffe's *The Romance of the Forest*, is set in France in the previous century. Not only is the work removed from English culture, but it also represents a farther step away from Milton and Bunyan. It shows how far literature had shifted in little over a century.

The novel contains a token cleric. He is no longer a messenger of repentance, as in Defoe's *Moll Flanders*. Rather, he represents kindly civility more than a dynamic spirituality. By the time of Radcliffe, nature had assumed a more significant role than previously. The novel is entitled *The Romance* of *the Forest* and not the merely *in* the forest. Nature takes on an aura evoking Burke's sublime: "The carriage drove along under the shade of 'melancholy boughs,' through which the evening twilight, which yet coloured the air, diffused a solemnity that vibrated in thrilling sensations upon the hearts of the travellers."[92] Radcliffe's novel can be seen as an early literary expression of the Romantic notion of nature as a symbol of the divine.

The Silent Revolution

As captured in the novels, eighteenth-century England was hearing competing voices. Often overlooked is the fact that England was expe-

---

91 William Cowper, "There Is a Fountain Filled with Blood," ahttp://www.cyberhymnal.org/htm/t/f/tfountfb.htm
92 Ann Radcliffe, *The Romance of the Forest*, ed. Chloe Chard (Oxford and New York: Oxford Unviersity Press, 1986), 14.

riencing a spiritual revolution. Herbert Schlossberg calls it the "silent revolution" that was to set the stage for the next century:

> the importance of Christianity in the West cannot really be very well understood by the historian who draws his information exclusively from documents. It lies rather in the constant preaching to the multitudes—often illiterate multitudes—of love and humility week after week in such a way that how people feel, think, and behave is vastly different than it otherwise would have been. [93]

Preachers were spreading the Gospel, and women such as Hannah More devoted their lives to it.[94] Phillis Wheatley (1753-84) became famous on both sides of the Atlantic. Born in Africa, this former slave became a spokesperson for American independence, abolition, and the Gospel; her poetry praised General George Washington (whom she later met, in 1776, and who was a fellow Christian), and she wrote a eulogy of George Whitefield, a portion of which declares:

> He offer'd THAT he did himself receive,
>
> A greater gift not GOD himself can give:
>
> He urg'd the need of HIM to every one;
>
> It was no less than GOD's co-equal SON!
>
> Take HIM ye wretched for your only good;
>
> Take HIM ye starving souls to be your food.
>
> Ye thirsty, come to this life giving stream:
>
> Ye Preachers, take him for your joyful theme:
>
> Take HIM, "my dear AMERICANS," he said,
>
> Be your complaints in his kind bosom laid:
>
> Take HIM ye Africans, he longs for you;
>
> Impartial SAVIOUR, is his title due;
>
> If you will chuse to walk in grace's road,
>
> You shall be sons, and kings, and priests to GOD.[95]

THE KANTIAN REVOLUTION

Wherever Protestantism had spread, it took on various traits as it took root, flourished, and became established in different lands. In France, it was relatively short-lived; following the religious wars, Voltaire and the *philosophes* looked for the downfall of Christianity. The Church of England was a compromise with politics; theology gave way to deism and latitudinarianism.

---
93   Herbert Schlossberg, *The Silent Revolution & the Making of Victorian England* (Columbus: Ohio State University Press, 2000), 288.
94   See Gordon Rupp, *Religion in England 1688-1791* (Oxford: Clarendon, 1986), 528-39.
95   "Poems on the revivalists of the Great Awakening," National Humanities Center Resource Toolbox, http://nationalhumanitiescenter.org/pds/becomingamer/ideas/text2/poemsevangelists.pdf

In Germany, the birthplace of the Reformation, the Pietist movement developed under Philipp Jacob Spener (1635-1705) and his disciple August Hermann Francke (1663-1727). Reacting against the dead orthodoxy of many churches and the widening gap between a highly professionalized clergy and the laity, Pietism sought to return to a simple religion of the heart. Some have seen the Enlightenment as an offshoot of Pietism; it is perhaps better to view the two as parallel movements. The German Immanuel Kant (1724-1804) attempted to integrate the two.

In his answer to the question "What is enlightenment?" Kant wrote, "Enlightenment is man's exit from his self-incurred minority" (8:35).[96] He explained that self-incurred minority was the "incapacity to use one's intelligence without the guidance of another" (9:35). Not through lack of intelligence, but through laziness and cowardice, most of mankind had looked to "alien guidance" rather than to its own powers of reason. *Sapere Aude!*—Dare to know—was the motto of the Enlightenment. Alongside Kant's emphasis on reason ran a lifelong concern with morality.

The First *Critique* and the Salvation of Philosophy

The starting point for Kant's philosophy is his so-called Copernican revolution. In his Preface to the Second Edition of the *Critique of Pure Reason*, Kant spoke of it as "assuming that the objects must conform to our cognition" rather than the other way around (B xvi).[97] Kant explained, "This would be just like the first thoughts of Copernicus," who developed his heliocentric system by shifting to a different vantage point for the human being. In declaring that the object conforms to the perceiver, Kant parallels Milton's attempt to "justify the ways of God to man" and Pope's "The proper study of mankind is Man."

For Kant, the new perception meant saving philosophy from skepticism. The British Empiricist David Hume had no room for a philosophy that did not deal with what can be analytically established or empirically tested. Kant pointed out that Hume had not considered all the options. And he allowed that certain legitimate areas of human endeavor lie outside the boundaries of pure reason. Much of the first *Critique* had been aimed at the concept of the autonomy of the individual thinking human being. Rather than being a mere passive recipient of sensory input, the mind interacts with and upon the outside world. Kant established the idea of schemata, a necessary link between intuition and pure concepts. Exactly how schematism works, Kant acknowledges, "is hidden in the depths of the human soul" (B 180-1).

---

96   Immanuel Kant, *Answer to the Question: What Is Enlightenment?* trans. Thomas K. Abbott in *Basic Writings of Kant*, ed. Allen W. Wood (New York: Modern Library, 2001), 135. Subsequent references to *What Is Enlightenment?* are from this edition.

97   Immanuel Kant, *Critique of Pure Reason*, trans. Paul Guyer (New York: Cambridge University Press, 1999). Subsequent references to this work are given in the text.

In showing the limitations of reason, Kant set the boundaries of the Enlightenment. For Hume metaphysical questions—e.g., concerning the soul—had been outside the realm of intelligible discussion. Hume's devotion to reason involved religious skepticism, as seen in his *Of Miracles and the Origin of Religion,* in which he questioned the miracles of the Bible. Kant was able to avoid Hume's skepticism, and at first it appears Kant had not only saved philosophy from skepticism, but also had opened the door for faith.

The Second *Critique*, Faith and the Centrality of Morality

The transition from the *Critique of Pure Reason* into his second *Critique,* which deals with practical reason, marks a movement toward the center of Kant's entire project—the moral law. Just as it was necessary to establish the autonomy of *reason* interacting with the world of objects, so it is now vital to demonstrate the autonomy of the *will* in moral action. Kant sees man as the center both of thought and action, in particular moral action. Man's decision-making process—the will—must be free, or the very idea of the moral law becomes meaningless.

Kant was trying to offer a philosophical rationale and replacement for the theological concept of the moral law, at times called the natural law. A chief Biblical text for this is Romans 2:14-15:

> Indeed, then Gentiles, who do not have the law [i.e., the written Mosaic law], do by nature things required by the law, they are a law for themselves, even though they do not have the law, since they show that the requirements of the law are written on their hearts, their consciences also bearing witness, and their thoughts now accusing, now even defending them.

Both the classic Christian doctrine of the moral law and Kant see the individual as having a moral sensibility. Yet there are significant differences; in Paul's expression in the Romans passage, the moral law is simply "written on [people's] hearts." Kant will not settle for such straightforward assertions; in his system, the individual must arrive at the moral law through the use of reason, which involves the Categorical Imperative: "So act that the maxim of your will could always hold at the same time as a principle in the giving of universal law" (5:30).[98]

Kant emphasizes that while freedom cannot be accounted for in pure reason, it is a *sine qua non* of practical reason and morality. On the one hand, pure reason calls for an acknowledgement of causality. On the other, practical reason means that we must have free will.

---

[98] Immanuel Kant, *Critique of Practical Reason,* in *Practical Philosophy,* ed. Mary J. Gregor (New York: Cambridge University Press, 1997), 164. Subsequent references to this work are given in the text.

Kant and Lutheran Theology

Throughout his writings, Kant was concerned not only with philosophical and moral issues, but with theological issues as well. Nevertheless, he had relatively little to say about Lutheran theology. While good works played a role in the Christian life, they were, according to Lutheran theology, a fruit of faith and not looked upon as a source of salvation. Moreover, the reformers looked to Scripture and placed it above reason in spiritual matters. Not so for Kant.

Kant came from a Lutheran Pietist family. Bernard Reardon points out the relation between such a background and rationalism: "What pietism and rationalism had in common, then, was the conviction that the meaning and value of Christianity lie in its practical ethic."[99] While Kant had bad memories from his Pietist school days, he always respected the simple faith of Pietism.

Living in the land of Luther, it is striking how little Kant dealt with the Gospel (grace) and its contrast with the Law, that is, the moral side of religion, especially since the Law-Gospel relationship is the center of Lutheran theology. Yet it is entirely consistent with Kant's project. Starting as he does with his Copernican revolution, his system cannot allow for the Gospel, any more than it has room for the concept of revealed religion that is not within the bounds of reason. For Kant, Christ becomes "the personified idea of the good principle" (6:60) and "it is our universal human duty to *elevate* ourselves to this ideal of moral perfection" (6:61).

While he may have left the door open for a rational faith—thus preserving the idea of God—in the end, it is a faith that continually needs to be reined in by reason. When all is said and done, Kant has displaced all three of the Reformation pillars—*sola scriptura, sola gratia, sola fide*. In their place he offers reason, morality, and a rational faith.

Beyond the Enlightenment

Since the early days of the Enlightenment, the intellectual history of Western civilization has largely been the attempt to find a worldview—*eine Weltanschauung*—to replace that of Christianity. In one way or another, the French *philosophes* and British Empiricists sought it in empirical knowledge. Kant saw that a knowledge based in the outside world could only lead to skepticism, as had been the case with Hume and others.

In the Appendix to his *Critique of Judgment* (1793), Kant anticipates Darwin and makes frequent reference to the theory of evolution. While his point is to establish freedom in nature, a concept vital to Kant's

---

99 Bernard M. G. Reardon, *Kant as Philosophical Theologian* (London: MacMillan, 1988), 16.

understanding of morality, the idea of evolution fits nicely with his doctrine of the progress of civilization.

Kant's later writings have been interpreted both as pantheistic and as atheistic. A quotation from one of those writings indicates why that should be the case: "Neither gods nor worlds exist but the *totality* of beings is God and world."[100] When one's God is not allowed to exceed the limits of a philosophical system, is not this what God must be—the sum of the world, which is either pantheism (all is God) or atheism (nothing is God)?

Much of Western civilization has followed those two branches. In one, both capitalism and atheistic communism have tended to replace spiritual with material concerns. In the other, New England Transcendentalism (named after Kant's Transcendental Idealism) led to the New Age Movement, grounded in pantheistic monism. We live in the legacy of the Kantian Revolution.

WILLIAM CAREY AND THE EXPANSION OF CHRISTIANITY

At the very time Christian faith was under assault from rationalism, it would experience an unprecedented worldwide expansion. After centuries of little missionary activity, the Reformation had paved the way for renewed interest in missions: "The roots of modern missions reach back to the Reformation in the very real sense that a revival of apostolic faith was the necessary precursor of a revival of apostolic life and work."[101]

There were some mission societies, such as among the German Moravians under Nikolaus Ludwig von Zinzendorf (1700-60), and the "Society for the Propagation of the Gospel in New England," organized in England in 1649. Yet there was also much indifference and apathy. William Carey, the "father of modern missions," would change all that.

Life in England (1761-92)

Carey was born in the village of Paulerspury, England. Because his father became parish clerk, he had access to books. At the age of twelve he taught himself Latin. His childhood interests in botany, languages, and foreign cultures were to stay with Carey throughout his life. At fourteen or sixteen, Carey became an apprentice shoemaker. He had been raised in the Anglican Church, but the senior apprentice with whom he worked was a Dissenter. About this time he began teaching himself Greek, the original language of the New Testament.

---

100 Hendrikus, Berkhof, *Two Hundred Years of Theology: Report of a Personal Journey*, trans. John Vriend (Grand Rapids: Eerdmans, 1989), 16.
101 Robert Hall Glover, "Period of the Early Missionary Societies," chapter VII in *The Progress of World-Wide Missions*, (New York: Harper, 1960), 45.

In 1781 Carey married Dorothy (Dolly) Plackett. This marriage began well enough but was not to remain happy. The first child of this union died in infancy. More grief would come. Within a year of his marriage Carey began preaching in a poor church. During this period he began to think of missions, having read of the voyages of Captain Cook and been influenced by David Brainerd (1718-47), a Scottish missionary to Indians in New England.

In 1787 Carey was ordained in the village of Olney, the home of hymnist William Cowper. Now Carey was becoming obsessed with the thought of missions. This was contrary to the "Particular Baptists" who maintained that "God would enlighten the heathen in his own way without human aid"[102] and the moderates who argued that "the evangelization of the heathen was the personal privilege of the Apostles; that the work had been fulfilled in previous ages."[103]

The Birth of Modern Missions (1792-93)

Carey's zeal for missions had become a white-hot flame when in May 1792 he published "An Enquiry into the Obligation of Christians to use means for the Conversion of the Heathens . . ." Among other things, he foresaw indigenous church workers. The immediate purpose of his "Enquiry" was in preparation for the meeting of the Baptist Association. On May 31, 1792 Carey preached to this humble assembly; his text was Isaiah 54:2,3: "Enlarge the place of thy tent . . ." He made the challenge, "Expect great things from God. Attempt great things for God."

The seed had been sown. In October, what was to become the Baptist Missionary Society was established. The first questions facing the society were "Whom do we send?" and "Where?" Enter John Thomas, who had spent some time in India as a self-appointed missionary. His enthusiasm moved Carey to volunteer to accompany him back to India, although Carey had dreamed of going to the South Seas.

Carey's parting words were, "Yonder in India is a gold mine. I will descend and dig, but you at home must hold the ropes."[104] The venture was difficult from the start. At first Carey's wife refused to go. When he learned of the plans, his father exclaimed, "Is William mad?" And the missionaries were not allowed to sail on a British ship. Eventually Dolly was persuaded, and the group found passage on a Danish ship. On 11 November 1793 they arrived in Calcutta, India, after five stormy months at sea. Carey said: "I feel something of what Paul felt when he beheld Athens, and 'his spirit was stirred within him.'"[105] He would never again see England.

---

102   Mary Drewery, *William Carey: a Biography* (Grand Rapids, MI: Zondervan, 1979),31.
103   Drewery, *William Carey: a Biography,* 31.
104   Glover, *The Progress of World-Wide Missions,* 61.
105   George Smith, *The Life of William Carey,* (New York: E. P. Dutton, 1909), 47.

Early Years in India (1793-99)

No welcome awaited Thomas, Carey, and his family. Instead, they were greeted with one discouragement after another: heat, dysentery, ignorance (theirs and the natives'), lack of funds, and the Hindu caste system. Thomas proved fickle. For a time he deserted the mission for his medical practice. Then he entered the "sugar trade," a euphemism for the distillation of rum.

Dolly began to sink into depression; their five year old son died; from this point on she was insane. For the last dozen years of her life, he cared for her at home. Carey supported his family by managing indigo factories in northern Bengal. Yet none of the workers responded favorably to his witnessing. Correspondence from England was infrequent. Funds were rare.

But Carey had a gift: the gift of persistence. Later in life, he said, "I can plod. I can persevere in any definite pursuit. To this I owe everything."[106] The early years in India were discouraging. Finally, in 1799, that began to change. That year two more workers arrived from England.

Success at Last (1800-01)

In January 1800 Carey joined them in the Danish settlement of Serampore. At this time the missionaries still had to avoid British areas. The British East India Company frowned on mission work lest it disturb the natives and upset trade. On the third last day of 1800, the first Indian convert was baptized in the Ganges River. The man's name was Krishna Pal; he later did mission work among his countrymen and wrote some hymns.

This baptism was followed by others. The numbers were never overwhelming (peaking at 174 baptisms in 1817); but the mission gradually grew. It was not from the number of converts that the fame of the "Serampore Trio" began to spread. Rather, it was from their linguistic ability, particularly that of Carey. With the help of Indian pundits, the Serampore missionaries translated the entire Bible into Bengali, Oriya, Marathi, Hindi, Assamese, and Sanskrit. Between 1801 and 1832 the Serampore Press printed 212,000 volumes in forty languages. Along with translating the Bible, Carey and his associates produced grammars, dictionaries, translations of Hindu writings into English, and periodicals in English and Bengali.

The "Plodder" (1802-14)

In the years following his first successes, Carey continued to "plod" along. A typical day of work—from six in the morning till nine at

---
106 Drewery, *William Carey: a Biography*, 25.

night—included translation, teaching, preaching, language study, publishing, and correspondence. After Dorothy Carey died, in December 1807, Carey remarried. Drawing on his experiences, Carey emphasized the importance of the missionary's wife. The year 1813 marked a change in British attitudes toward missionaries. Thanks much to the efforts of William Wilberforce, they now had official government approval.

Trials (1815-28)

After enjoying the fruits of his labors for about a dozen years, Carey was now to enter into another dozen years of progress. But these years were mixed with severe trials. In 1815 the mission's chief support back in England, Andrew Fuller, died. With his death the relationship between mission and home weakened. Then came more deaths: his wife, Krisha Pal, his oldest son and helper Felix, and the last of the British trio.

About this time the mission began to meet another type of opposition. A Bengali intellectual, Ram Mohun Roy (1772-1833), began to publish articles defending Hinduism and attacking Christian doctrines, especially the Trinity. Roy did much to revive people's interest in their own religion; he is considered a prime mover in the modern revival and reform of Hinduism.

Yet Carey kept plodding. Serampore College opened in 1819, with the purpose of training Indians to replace Europeans as missionaries and create an indigenous church. This institute is still open. In 1823 Carey married a widow; this marriage was also a good one.

Final Years (1829-34)

Carey's last years were crowned with a number of joys. In 1829 the British government outlawed the practice of *sati*, the burning of widows along with their husbands. After decades of trying to get it outlawed, Carey was probably the one person most responsible for its abolition. He also did much to outlaw infanticide and also spoke out against slavery, self-torture, and the entire caste system.

Toward the end of his life Carey was visited by a steady stream of guests, including British government officials, Anglican dignitaries, Indian leaders, scholars, and missionaries. One of his last visitors was the famous Scottish missionary Alexander Duff. As Carey lay on his deathbed Duff praised his numerous achievements. To which the dying man softly replied, "Mr. Duff, you have been speaking about Dr. Carey, Dr. Carey; when I am gone, say nothing about Dr. Carey—speak about

Dr. Carey's Saviour."[107] Carey was buried next to his second wife. The inscription beneath his name had been chosen by the missionary:

WILLIAM CAREY

Born August 17th, 1761

Died June 9th, 1834

"A wretched, poor and helpless worm

On Thy kind arms I fall."

---

[107] Walter Bruce Davis, *William Carey—Father of Modern Missions* (Chicago: Moody Press, 1963), 104.

PART 3
THE AGE OF ROMANTICISM: 1800 — 1850

THE EARLY ROMANTICS

Romantic Stirrings

> The breezy call of incense-breathing morn,
> The swallow twitt'ring from the straw-built shed,
> The cock's shrill clarion, or the echoing horn,
> No more shall rouse them from their lowly bed.[108]

Published in 1751, Thomas Gray's *Elegy Written in a Country Churchyard,* was an early expression of a literary movement taking place in England. The Enlightenment had taken hold but seemed to bring with it an almost immediate longing for more. Gray's poem expresses that longing. Meanwhile, in Germany, Johann Wolfgang von Goethe (1749-1832) and the *Sturm und Drang* (storm and stress) movement gave renewed emphasis to emotional longings.

About this time, the Industrial Revolution initiated a period of growth in the British economy and with it the growth of cities. London and other cities were becoming manufacturing centers. The changing economics affected work patterns, which affected church attendance: "People were less willing, or more probably less able, because of their changing work routines, to attend weekday services and lectures."[109] Yet Britain continued in its Christian tradition.

It was the Christian consciousness that continued to work much good, including the end to slavery. Enlightenment philosophers had expressed mixed attitudes toward the subject. Hume's was negative, "I am apt to suspect the Negroes and in general all other species of men . . . to be naturally inferior to the whites."[110] And Kant followed suit, "The Ne-

---

108 From Thomas Gray's, *Elegy Written in a Country Churchyard,* as quoted in Albert, *A Short History of English Literature,* 74.
109 Jacob, *Lay People and Religion in the Early Eighteenth Century,* 228.
110 David Hume, "Negroes Naturally Inferior to the Whites," in Kramnick, *The Portable Enlightenment Reader,* 629.

groes of Africa have by nature no feeling that rises above the trifling."[111] It took dedicated Christians such as the former slave Olaudah Equiano (1745-97), Hannah More, and her friend William Wilberforce to bring change. A member of parliament, Wilberforce (1759-1833) led the fight to abolish the slave trade, culminating in the Slave Trade Act and the Slavery Abolition Act.

For the most part, however, the Romantic Age is associated with the continuing drift away from the faith. Midway between Milton and today stood Romanticism, which in England was dominated by the poets Wordsworth, Coleridge, Blake, Keats, Shelley, and Byron. Among the first three—the "early" Romantics—we still see, as Wordsworth put it, "affinities between religion and poetry."[112] By the end of the Romantic period, that affinity was transformed.

William Wordsworth and Samuel Taylor Coleridge

Wordsworth (1770-1850) was the poet of nature and committed himself to a "marriage between mind and nature."[113] His work is shot through a heightened consciousness "of splendor in the grass, of glory in the flower."[114] For Wordsworth, nature took on a "morally educative influence,"[115] and children, who are closer to nature, teach adults:

> My heart leaps up when I behold
>
> A rainbow in the sky:
>
> So was it when my life began;
>
> So is it now I am a man;
>
> So be it when I shall grow old,
>
> Or let me die!
>
> The Child is father of the Man;
>
> And I could wish my days to be
>
> Bound each to each by natural piety.[116]

Lyrical Ballads, which Wordsworth co-published with Coleridge in 1798, is considered *the* work that ushered in the Romantic Movement. It concludes with the lengthy poem written in England's Lake District, "Lines Composed a Few Miles above Tintern Abbey, on Revisiting the Banks of the Wye during a Tour." Toward the end of the work, the poet exclaims to his sister:

---

111 Immanuel Kant, "The Differences between the Races," in Kramnick, *The Portable Enlightenment Reader,* 638.
112 As quoted in M. H. Abrams, *Natural Supernaturalism: Tradition and Revolution in Romantic Literature* (New York: and London: W. W. Norton, 1971), 394.
113 Abrams, *Natural Supernaturalism,* 27.
114 William Wordsworth, *Ode: Intimations of Immortality,* in *Selected Poems,* ed. John O. Hayden (New York: Penguin Books, 1994), 144.
115 Sanders, *The Short Oxford History of English Literature,* 359.
116 Wordsworth, *My Heart Leaps up When I Behold,* in *Selected Poems,* 138.

> Wilt thou then forget
> That on the banks of this delightful stream
> We stood together; and that I, so long
> A worshipper of Nature, hither came
> Unwearied in that service:[117]

In the *Preface to the Second Edition of Lyrical Ballads,* the "worshipper of Nature" discusses the break from the lofty language of neo-classical poetry, and the quest to write about "common life" in "language really used by men."[118] In developing an art for average people, not just for the elite, he set feelings on center stage—the feeling "gives importance to the action and situation, and not the action and situation to the feeling."[119] Whereas earlier poets had described external events, Wordsworth describes interior feelings. Art has moved from being a mirror of the external world (mimesis) to a lamp emanating from within.

For Coleridge (1772-1834), as for other Romantics, this creative act of the artist was analogous with the creative act of God.[120] Among the Romantics, Coleridge was uniquely aware of German higher criticism of the Bible. Moved by his studies, he sought to "free Christianity from fundamentalism."[121] Like Wordsworth, he turned to nature for inspiration:

> It may indeed be fantasy, when I
> Essay to draw from all created things
> Deep, heartfelt, inward joy that closely clings;
> And trace in leaves and flowers that round me lie
> Lessons of love and earnest piety.[122]

Later in life, both poets turned to Biblical faith. Coleridge wrote his own Epitaph:

> Stop, Christian passer-by!—Stop, child of God,
> And read with gentle breast. Beneath this sod
> A poet lies, or that which once seem'd he . . .
> Mercy for praise—to be forgiven for fame
> He ask'd, and hoped, through Christ. Do thou the same![123]

The fact that there was a church still holding to the old Christian values is significant. The spiritual climate of England was still largely "imbued with Evangelicalism."[124]

---

117 Wordsworth, *Selected Poems*, 70.
118 William Wordsworth, Preface to the Second Edition of Lyrical Ballads, in Adams, *Critical Theory since Plato*, 438.
119 Wordsworth, Preface to the Second Edition of Lyrical Ballads, 439.
120 See, for example, Samuel Taylor Coleridge, *Biographia Literaria*, in Adams, *Critical Theory since Plato*, 477.
121 Sanders, *The Short Oxford History of English Literature*, 365.
122 Samuel Taylor Coleridge, *To Nature*, in *The Portable Coleridge*, ed. I. A. Richards (New York: Penguin Books, 1978), 204.
123 Coleridge, *To Nature*, in *The Portable Coleridge*, 216.
124 Sanders, *The Short Oxford History of English Literature*, 366.

William Blake

The third of the early Romantics, William Blake (1757-1827) is another story. Raised in a dissenting family, Blake knew the Bible well. Indeed, it was the most important influence on his life. Blake rejected the nature religion of Wordsworth and Coleridge; nevertheless, although Blake used biblical imagery, he departed from historic Christian thought. He developed in effect his own religion. Blake was at odds both with the Enlightenment idea that nature and reason are in harmony and with the Romantic notion that nature educates and even teaches moral values.[125] In keeping with Enlightenment thought, Blake felt that man is the measure—not, however, through reason, but through the imagination, that is, the poetic or prophetic genius.

He saw the established church, along with the government of his day, as corrupt. Those powers, in Blake's view, bore the mark of the beast, a term connected with the Anti-Christ in Revelation 13. Moreover, the Anglican Church of Blake's day was "dominated by deism."[126]

Blake and his wife showed brief interest in Swedenborg's ideas, attending at least the first session of a five-day conference in 1789.[127] Blake appreciated Swedenborg's ideas, but he did not like the fact that the Swedenborgians had set up another church. Moreover, in *The Marriage of Heaven and Hell,* he parted ways with Swedenborg's thought: "he has not written one new truth . . . he has written all the old falsehoods" (Plate 22).[128] According to Blake, Swedenborg's main error was his acceptance of conventional morality: In the *Marriage*, Blake aligned more with influences like the medieval occultist Paracelsus, the German theosophist Jakob Boehme, and pagan sources. Although he reacted against established religion and set himself somewhat apart from radical religious thought, he was not an advocate of a simple return to the Bible.

In Blake's fallen world, reason rules with an oppressive tyranny. John Beer points out that like Wordsworth and Coleridge, Blake "saw the problem" raised by the Age of Reason, namely, "a rationalist view of man."[129] Blake's *The Book of Urizen* deals with this issue. Urizen ("Your reason") represents the autocratic rule of reason, embodied in church and government.

Blake opposed dualism. His opposition included the Bible with its spirit-body, heaven-hell, good-evil, and—perhaps, above all—law-gospel dualisms. In the unfinished poem, *The Everlasting Gospel* (1818 or later), he wrote:

---

125 William Blake, *The Complete Poetry and Prose of William Blake*, ed. David V. Erdman (New York: Doubleday, 1988), 2.
126 Kathleen Raine, *Blake and the New Age* (London: George Allen and Unwin, 1979), 32.
127 David V. Erdman, *Blake: Prophet Against Empire* (New York: Dover, 1977), 143.
128 William Blake, *Blake's Poetry and Designs*, ed. Mary Lynn Johnson and John E. Grant (New York and London: Norton, 1979), 98. Subsequent Blake quotations are from this edition, with page or plate numbers in parentheses.
129 John Beer, *Blake's Visionary Universe* (New York: Barnes and Noble, 1969), 6.

> Good & Evil are no more!
> Sinai's trumpets cease to roar! (370)

This is clearly antinomian. It harmonizes with *The Marriage of Heaven and Hell*:

> Now hear how [Jesus] has given his sanction to the law of ten commandments: did he not mock at the sabbath, and so mock the sabbath's God? murder those who were murdered because of him? turn away the law from the woman taken in adultery? steal the labor of others to support him? bear false witness when he omitted making a defence before Pilate? covet when he prayed for his disciples, and when he bid them shake off the dust of their feet against such as refused to lodge them? I tell you, no virtue can exist without breaking these ten commandments. Jesus was all virtue, and acted from impulse not from rules. (Plates 23-24)

But in fact, Jesus did not act from impulse. He kept the law perfectly. Most of what Blake here referred to as the Ten Commandments were Pharisaical accretions to the law. To note but the first example, that of the Sabbath, Luke records how "on the Sabbath day he [Jesus] went into the synagogue, as was his custom" (4:16). This was in keeping with the commandment, "Remember the Sabbath day by keeping it holy" (Exodus 20:8).

Jerusalem (1804) is William Blake's grandest creation, a poem with 100 engraved plates and more than 4000 lines. In *Jerusalem,* Blake took up the notion of those dissenters who saw Jerusalem as being rebuilt in England. A point of contact between *Jerusalem* and Scripture is the person of Jesus Christ, the *anointed* Messiah (Greek, *Christos*) promised in the Old Testament and the one who would *save* his people from their sins (Greek, *Iesous*). *Jerusalem* carries the superscription Μονος ο Ιησους, "Jesus alone," from John 8:1-11, the story of the woman caught in adultery. When the people were about to stone her to death, Jesus confronted them, "If any of you is without sin, let him be the first to throw a stone at her." Then he looked down and wrote something on the ground. The text goes on to relate what happened when he looked up:

> . . . only Jesus was left, with the woman standing there. Jesus straightened up and asked her, "Woman, where are they? Has no one condemned you?"
>
> "No one, sir," she said.
>
> "Then neither do I condemn you," Jesus declared. "Go now and leave your life of sin."

In his introduction to the first chapter of *Jerusalem*, Blake writes, "The Spirit of Jesus is continual forgiveness of Sin: he who waits to be righteous before he enters into the Saviour's kingdom . . . will never enter there. I am perhaps the most sinful of men!" (312) Like the Bible, Blake connected Jesus closely with forgiveness. Blake, however, evidences a gnostic concept of evil, in that he exalts knowledge (*gnosis*) above the problem of good and evil:

> I care not whether a Man is good or Evil; all that I care
> Is whether he is a Wise Man or a Fool. (Plate 91:54-5)

In the Biblical account of Jesus forgiving the woman, the final verse says: "Go now, and leave your life of sin." The Biblical doctrine of grace does not suggest overlooking sin. Rather, it includes the payment for sin (the Lamb sacrificially shedding his blood). Forgiveness is accompanied by a desire to live according to God's will (see Romans 6:1-4).

Blake's concept of sin and forgiveness also differed from that of his contemporary John Newton (1725-1807). A rector in the Church of England and a former slave trader, Newton wrote one of the most beloved hymns of all time:

> Amazing grace—how sweet the sound—
> That saved a wretch like me!
> I once was lost but now am found,
> Was blind but now I see.[130]

Blake's writing breathes the language of the Scriptures, yet there is a different spirit at work. His work is human-centered and lacks a doctrine of a transcendent God. Throughout Blake's work, his view of God remained unsettled. His opposition to dualism led him on an endless search for some sort of resolution of contraries. It pushed him toward an Eastern, monistic view of life—one thinks of his repeated phrase "everything that lives is Holy."[131] For Blake, the free use of the imagination (the "Divine-Humanity," *Jerusalem,* Plate 70:19) is the goal of religion. He lived by the fruit of his imagination and died "singing about what he saw in heaven."[132]

THE LATER ROMANTICS

"[God] has made everything beautiful in its time. He has also set eternity in the hearts of men" (Ecclesiastes 3:11).

Despite the Romantics' move toward a non-Biblical, secular, human-centered view of life, the longing to transcend this world (*saeculum*) and touch something of the eternal remained. A look at the later Romantics underscores this fact. As Ecclesiastes says, the longing for that which transcends life's passing moment lies deep within the human soul. It is as old as death itself. For the later Romantics, the longing to transcend this life remained, but the meaning of transcendence changed.

---

130   C. T. Aufdemberge, *Christian Worship: Handbook* (Milwaukee: Northwestern, 1997), 397.
131   *Visions of Albion* (Plate 8); *America* (Plate 8:13); *The Marriage of Heaven and Hell* (Plate 25).
132   Blake, *Blake's Poetry and Designs,* xxxviii.

John Keats and a Thing of Beauty

"A thing of beauty is a joy for ever,"[133] wrote the twenty-two-year-old John Keats (1795-1821). It was the same year that Keats bowed to a likeness of Voltaire "in preference to one of Christ."[134] Keats was a rationalist, and his rationalism had led him to see beauty as truth itself and to find therein a sense of permanence. This was Keats's thought; it was his religion.

The essence of Keats's work is captured in two representative odes, both written in 1819. In one, *Ode to a Nightingale*, he approached the matter of transcendence through nature. In the other, *Ode to the Grecian Urn*, he did it through art.

Ode to a Nightingale might be considered an expression of Keats's longing, for "a revival of the original 'natural religion' to which the Christianity of Keats's day seemed to be giving way."[135] The poem opens with a deep sense of longing:

> My heart aches, and a drowsy numbness pains
> My sense, as though of hemlock I had drunk . . .

Surrounded by "mid-May's" luxuriant, yet quickly fading growth, the poet listens . . . and waits, "half in love with easeful death," aware that even when he has "become a sod," the bird will sing on: "Thou wast not born for death, immortal Bird!"

Interestingly, Keats did include a Biblical allusion in the stanza about the immortal bird:

> Perhaps the self-same song that found a path
> Through the sad heart of Ruth, when, sick for home,
> She stood in tears amid the alien corn.

In the Biblical account, the Moabite Ruth felt no such sadness and was quite happy to follow her Hebrew mother-in-law Naomi to her land. As Ruth vowed, "Your people will be my people and your God my God" (Ruth 1:16), and it was amid the alien corn that she met her husband Boaz. In light of Keats's general attitude toward Christianity, his poetic license in this passing allusion might be construed as indifference to the Scriptures. Keats did indeed imbibe the skepticism of his day, which was "the most important intellectual problem of . . . the age of romanticism."[136]

---

133   Keats quotations are from John Keats, *Complete Poems*, ed. Jack Stillinger (Cambridge, MA and London: Belknap Press of Harvard University Press, 1982).
134   Robert M. Ryan, *Keats: The Religious Sense* (Princeton, NJ: Princeton University Press, 1976), 185.
135   Ryan, *Keats: The Religious Sense*, 4.
136   C. E. Pulos, as quoted by Ronald A. Sharp, *Keats, Skepticism, and the Religion of Beauty* (Athens: University of Georgia Press, 1979), 12.

Keats closed "Ode to a Nightingale" on a dreamlike note:

> Was it a vision, or a waking dream?
> Fled is that music:—Do I wake or sleep?

Here, as often, Keats blurred the distinction between dream and reality. He needed to create a reality beyond the material, since for him the old transcendence was gone.

In *Ode on a Grecian Urn*, Keats tried for the same breakthrough as in *Nightingale*, but in a different setting. This time the poem takes us not into the world of nature but to classical Greece. The ode's final stanza closes with the thought that although people pass away, the urn remains:

> When old age shall this generation waste,
> Thou shalt remain, in midst of other woe
> Than ours, a friend to man, to whom thou say'st,
> "Beauty is truth, truth beauty,"—that is all
> Ye know on earth, and all ye need to know.

Keats sees beauty as truth that is beyond philosophical speculation but discovered through sensory experience and imagination.

Keats's longing for transcendence is connected with thoughts of beauty, youthfulness, and permanence. How successful was Keats in this creative quest? Stricken with tuberculosis, by the time he left Briton for the warmth of Italy in September 1820, he had not written poetry "for months."[137] In Italy, mental delirium accompanied physical hemorrhaging. When he died, at age twenty-five, on February 23, 1821, his last words to his friend Severn were, "Severn—Severn—lift me up for I am dying—I shall die easy—don't be frightened—thank God it has come."[138] It is doubtful Keats had experienced some sort of deathbed conversion. It is ironic that he should appeal to a deity he had spent a lifetime denying.

Shelley and the Unbinding of Prometheus

In 1811, the eighteen-year-old Percy Bysshe Shelley (1792-1822) was expelled from Oxford for publishing a pamphlet called *The Necessity of Atheism*. Actually the title was "more pugnacious than its contents."[139] Shelley was calling for the free investigation into religious beliefs and pointing out that God's existence is not proven. Since that time, the poet's name has been connected with atheism. "When asked years later why he called himself an atheist, he admitted that he used

---

[137] Timothy Hilton, *Keats and His World* (New York: Viking Press, 1971), 121.
[138] Hilton, *Keats and His World*, 126.
[139] Claire Tomalin, *Shelley and His World* (London: Thames and Hudson, 1980), 18.

the term for its effect."[140] On the other hand, to assert that "Shelley is in essence a Christian poet,"[141] one must stretch the definition of Christian to the breaking point. What brings him closest to Christianity, it seems, is his emphasis on love. Yet this hardly makes Shelley an advocate of Christianity.

Like Sir Philip Sidney two and a half centuries earlier, Shelley composed a prose essay defending poetry. Shelley's *A Defense of Poetry* was also published posthumously, in 1840. Moreover, Shelley harked back to poetry's role in the Bible as well as to its Greek and Roman roots. In such ways, Shelley stood in the "poetic tradition" of Sidney. But there were differences. While Shelley appealed to the classics and the Bible—and added sources since Sidney's time, namely, Shakespeare and Milton— the common ground had shifted. No longer did the poet feel compelled to speak of our Saviour Christ and of praising God. Rather, Shelley concluded, "Poets are the unacknowledged legislators of the world."[142]

Of all Shelley's works, none epitomizes his thought so magnificently as *Prometheus Unbound*. Among the Romantics, Shelley had the best mastery of Greek classics. His confidence as a classicist is evident in the freedom with which he changed the story of Prometheus to fit his purposes. In the old myth, Prometheus finally comes to terms with Zeus (Jupiter); in Shelley's version, Demogorgon defeats Zeus, whereupon Prometheus is freed.

Jupiter's defeat at the hands of Demogorgon is followed by the freeing of Prometheus and all of nature. In place of lovelessness or misdirected love, harmonious love now reigns. Act IV, which Shelley added as a nuptial song, celebrates the reunion of Prometheus and Asia. Here the Moon proclaims to the earth:

> Gazing on thee I feel, I know,
>
> Green stalks burst forth, and bright flowers grow
>
> And living shapes upon my bosom move:
>
> Music is in the sea and air,
>
> Winged clouds soar here and there,
>
> Dark with the rain new buds are dreaming of:
>
> 'Tis Love, all Love!

In the second half of the poem, we are presented with a vision of Shelley's paradise. It is a world of the imagination. Here, in this new world, we get a picture of how far the poet has moved from Milton's *Paradise Regained*. Shelley's paradise is a world brought about not by God's work of redemption, but by man. Mary Shelley said of the poem:

---
140 Bryan Shelley, *Shelley and Scripture: The Interpreting Angel* (Oxford: Clarendon, 1994), 17.
141 James O. Allsup, *The Magic Circle: A Study of Shelley's Concept of Love* (London: Kennikat, 1976), ix.
142 Percy Bysshe Shelley, *A Defense of Poetry*, in Adams, *Critical Theory since Plato*, 529.

> The prominent feature of Shelley's theory of the destiny of the human species was, that evil is not inherent in the system of the creation, but an accident that might be expelled.... That man could be so perfectionized as to be able to expel evil from his own nature, and from the greater part of creation, was the cardinal point of his system.[143]

The entire divine-human order has been reversed. It is the poet who is the judge of the divine.

Whereas Keats had explored the possibility of the individual attaining some sort of transcendence or immortality, Shelley was concerned with the possibility of redeeming society. To that end, Shelley has created a world of the imagination in which death is still a reality, but love rules. Institutions and the hatred they inspire are no more. The poem closes:

> To suffer woes which Hope thinks infinite;
>
> To forgive wrongs darker than Death or Night;
>
> To defy Power which seems Omnipotent;
>
> To love, and bear; to hope, till Hope creates
>
> From its own wreck the thing it contemplates;
>
> Neither to change nor falter nor repent:
>
> This, like thy glory, Titan! is to be
>
> Good, great and joyous, beautiful and free;
>
> This is alone Life, Joy, Empire and Victory.

The reality of the poet's life did not conform to this ideal. Shelley moved from one unsatisfying romantic fixation to the next, while becoming estranged from his wife. Three months before his death, Shelley lamented, "Alas, how I am fallen from the boasted purity in which you knew me once exulting!"[144] Weeks before his death by drowning off the coast of Italy, Shelley began his last work, *The Triumph of Life*. The poem ends without answering its final question:

> "Then what is Life?" I said ... the cripple cast
>
> His eye upon the car which now had rolled
>
> Onward, as if that look must be the last,
>
> And answered.... "Happy those for whom the fold
>
> Of

Like Keats, Shelley lives on in his work. Yet the utopian transcendence he sought eluded him.

---

143 As quoted in Allsup, *The Magic Circle*, 95f.
144 William D. Brewer, *The Shelley-Byron Conversation* (Gainesville: University Press of Florida, 1994), 130.

Manfred: the Byronic Man

If there were a nineteenth century rock star, it would have been the handsome, adventuresome, athletic, worldly, and brilliant George Gordon, Lord Byron (1788-1824). Ironically, of all the Romantics except Blake, it seems that Byron was most at home in the Scriptures. He "drew copiously upon Scripture . . . throughout his poetry."[145] This is clear from major works such as *Cain,* from shorter poems such as *The Destruction of Sennacherib,* and in the many almost matter-of-fact Biblical allusions scattered throughout his works. At the same time, Byron was the most materialistic of the Romantics. Perhaps more fully than the other poets, he recognized the implication of turning from the Bible. Hence we have the Byronic hero: proud, cynical, haunted by guilt, outcast from society, and isolated.

Nowhere is this more evident than in the dramatic poem *Manfred,* which "may be described as being the climax of the Byronic style and hero."[146] *Manfred* outraged Byron's contemporaries for its seeming avowal of his incestuous passion for his half-sister Augusta.[147] In the drama this incest becomes equivalent to murder, and the drama can be read as "a study in remorse," with Byron as Manfred, Augusta as Astarte, the various spirits as "anything one likes."[148] Whatever might be said of the drama, it is the story of the individual's longing for immortality.

The drama opens with Manfred alone in a Gothic gallery at midnight. He summons his own condemned star and attendant spirits. "He asks forgetfulness of self," notes Harold Bloom.[149] Manfred seems to seek more than that. In the conclusion of the first act, Manfred does, indeed, attempt to kill himself, only to be saved by the chamois hunter.

Manfred realizes that "in itself death will offer no solace"[150] He must come to terms with himself and find some inner peace. This comes through the appearance of Astarte's phantom:

PHANTOM OF ASTARTE. Manfred!

MAN.   Say on, say on—

         I live but in the sound—it is thy voice!

PHAN.   Manfred! To-morrow ends thine earthly ills.

         Farewell!

---

145 Wolf Z. Hirst, ed., *Byron, the Bible, and Religion: Essays from the Twelfth International Byron Seminar* (Newark: University of Delaware Press, 1985), 77. Some 1704 "uses of the Bible" have been found throughout Byron's poetry (136).
146 A. Craig Bell, *Byron: His Achievement and Significance* (Darley: The Grian-Aig Press, 1976), 46.
147 Bell, *Byron,* 47.
148 Bell, *Byron,* 47.
149 Harold Bloom, *The Visionary Company: A Reading of English Romantic Poetry* (Ithaca and London: Cornell University Press, 1971), 249.
150 William H. Marshall, *The Structure of Byron's Major Poems* (Philadelphia: University of Pennsylvania Press, 1962), 107.

MAN.   Yet one word more—am I forgiven?

PHAN.   Farewell![151]

In the drama's final dialogue, Manfred rejects the Christian comfort offered by the Abbot. Manfred's last words are a defiant farewell to the Abbot: "Old man! 'tis not so difficult to die." Byron saw these words as containing "the whole effect and moral of the poem."[152] For Manfred, transcendence has been a matter of the self-assertion of the human will. The egotistical Manfred seems to die unhumbled, thinking that in some way he has conquered even death itself.

In January 1824, Byron wrote "On This Day I Complete My Thirty-Sixth Year." It was to be one of the last things he wrote. Byron died as he had lived much of his life—lonely and defiant:

> My days are in the yellow leaf;
>
> > The flowers and fruits of love are gone;
>
> The worm—the canker, and the grief
>
> > Are mine alone!

The Poet's Work

Keats, Shelley, and Byron were not Christians. It is possible to attribute many of their negative attitudes toward the Christian faith to the state of English Christianity in their day. Robert Ryan has well described the church of the Romantic age:

> The second half of the eighteenth century had brought a steady decline in faith and piety among members of the Church . . . The age of reason had not provided a hospitable milieu for religious faith, and, although English theologians . . . effectively rebutted the attacks of the Deists from without, the critical spirit had made damaging incursions within the Church itself. . . . liberal ecclesiastics were disposed to gloss over difficult or controversial articles of faith and to emphasize instead those religious notions, such as the Fatherhood of God and the brotherhood of man, which all believers held in common. . . . The end product was a religion eminently reasonable by contemporary standards, but rather cold and colorless, offering little nourishment to the emotions or to the imagination.[153]

Under such circumstances, writers looked elsewhere than the church for their inspiration. Keats, Shelley, and Byron were not atheists, although Byron came as close as any of them to being a materialist. Rather, they were agnostics, seeking to find a new way. Bloom notes, "It is one of the great characteristics of the Romantic period that each major poet in turn sought to rival and surpass Milton, while also renewing his vision. To

---

151   Byron quotations are from George Gordon, Lord Byron, *Byron,* ed. Jerome J. McGann (Oxford and New York: Oxford University Press, 1986).
152   Bloom, *The Visionary Company,* 252.
153   Ryan, *Keats: The Religious Sense,* 16f.

surpass Milton in this context could only mean to correct his vision by humanizing it."[154]

In their attempts at "humanizing," Keats turned to beauty, Shelley to an ideal society, and Byron to the Byronic figure. Yet each experienced and projected in his work the longing of the human heart to transcend the human condition. In sloughing off Christian faith, the Romantics sought to liberate man. For this they gave up the personal hope of immortality, based so solidly in the Gospels' accounts of Jesus' resurrection.

AMERICAN ROMANTICISM: RALPH WALDO EMERSON

The American Scene

The movements that changed Europe in the eighteenth and nineteenth centuries also crossed the Atlantic, where the Enlightenment and Romanticism took on new shapes. "The form of the Enlightenment that prevailed in the United States," notes church historian Mark Noll, "was derived from an important school of Scottish thinkers known as 'common sense' philosophers":

> [T]hese Scots shared the general confidence of eighteenth century Europe that it was now possible to see the truth—moral physical, social—with greater clarity than in previous generations. They differed from other thinkers such as Hume and Voltaire, however, by showing how their Enlightenment thought could be compatible with at least the broad outline of received Christianity.[155]

During the transition from the Age of Reason to Romanticism and throughout the nineteenth century, the United States was a stronghold of Christian faith, in particular Protestantism. Historians refer to that period as the "Protestant Century." In the wake of the Revolutionary War, less than ten percent of the population held formal church membership,[156] but the Second Great Awakening (1795-1810) helped usher renewed vigor to the Christian churches.

By 1835, Alexis De Tocqueville would write in *Democracy in America*, "[T]here is no country in the world where the Christian religion retains a greater influence over the souls of men than in America . . . In France I had almost always seen the spirit of religion and the spirit of freedom marching in opposite directions. But in America I found they were intimately united and that they reigned in common over the same country."[157] That mix of Christian faith and love for country is

---
154 Bloom, *The Visionary Company*, xxiv.
155 Mark A. Noll, *A History of Christianity in the United States and Canada* (Grand Rapids: Eerdmans, 1992), 154.
156 Martin E. Marty, *Righteous Empire: The Protestant Experience in America* (New York: Dial Press, 1970), 169.
157 Mark A. Noll, et al., eds. *Eerdmans' Handbook to Christianity in America* (Grand Rapids: Eerdmans, 1983),

exemplified in the work of Francis Scott Key (1779-1843). In addition to penning "The Star-Spangled Banner," Key wrote the hymn "Before the Lord We Bow," which expresses trust in Christ, "heaven's high King" and the "great Redeemer":

> The nation Thou hast blest
>
> May well Thy love declare,
>
> From foes and fears at rest,
>
> Protected by Thy care.[158]

. . . .

Alongside a general Christian consensus—including the Bible as the bedrock of religious knowledge and social values—there ran another strain in American life. "For the first time a predominately Christian nation unfettered the church from state control and allowed different and competing manifestations of the church to operate freely. . . ."[159]

The lack of central religious authority and theologians trained in the original Biblical languages left Scripture wide open to the interpretation of everyone. Fragmentation of denominations and the formation of new groups became the order of the day. As de Tocqueville put it, "The Americans demanded that they were free, masterless individuals; they sought absolute independence and equality of status. They imagine that their whole destiny is in their own hands. . . . They acquire the habit of always imagining themselves as standing alone."[160] In this climate of rugged individualism and men of action, there was little room for the reflective theologian. Rather, the likes of "illiterate Methodist preachers . . . set the world on fire."[161]

It was only a matter of time before European secularizing thought would take root in American soil. The seeds were already present in a significant difference between the First Great Awakening (1730s-40s) and the Second. During the First Awakening, men such as Jonathan Edwards and George Whitefield had emphasized God's sovereignty and "the inability of sinful people to save themselves."[162] In the Second Awakening, preachers "suggested that God had bestowed on all people the ability to come to Christ."[163] This theological shift, which was also taking place at seminaries, was in keeping with the action-minded American mentality and mirrored the Arminian and Enlightenment shift from theo-centric to man-centered thought.

96-130
158 W. G. Polack, *The Handbook to the Lutheran Hymnal* (St. Louis: Concordia, 1958), 409.
159 Noll, *Eerdmans' Handbook to Christianity in America*, 208.
160 Noll, *Eerdmans' Handbook to Christianity in America*, 208.
161 Noll, *Eerdmans' Handbook to Christianity in America*, 210.
162 Noll, *A History of Christianity in the United States*, 170.
163 Noll, *A History of Christianity in the United States*, 170.

Ralph Waldo Emerson: Optimistic Visionary

Ralph Waldo Emerson (1803-82) is well known as an exponent of liberal theology in America. Much of what Emerson would articulate was already circulating among New England (and European) intelligentsia. In 1807, "in protest against Harvard College's drift toward Unitarianism,"[164] a group of Trinitarian Congregationalists founded Andover Theological Seminary, the nation's first full-fledged institution for theological education.

In 1822, the noted theologian Nathaniel William Taylor became the first professor at the Yale Divinity School. He was a champion in the fight against Unitarianism in New England. But liberal theologians were not to be denied. Among them was William Ellery Channing, who held the pulpit of Boston's Federal Street Congregational Church from 1803 until his death in 1842. Channing set forth the tenets of Unitarianism, denying the Trinity, the deity of Christ, the total depravity of human beings, and the substitutionary atonement of Jesus. By the early 1820s, liberalism in the form of Unitarianism had made strong inroads in New England, and beyond.

Emerson was much influenced by Channing's "reverence for human nature and man's free will."[165] Emerson also saw modern science in conflict with what he called "historical Christianity." In 1832, he told his congregation, "I regard it as the irresistible effect of the Copernican astronomy to have made the theological scheme of redemption absolutely incredible."[166] Eventually, even Unitarianism would be too confining for Emerson. Influenced by such disparate sources as Kant (from whom the term transcendental came), Schleiermacher, Goethe, Jacob Boehme, Swedenborg, and Hinduism, Emerson and others formed the Transcendental Club in 1836. While Unitarianism saw man "with inherent worth who controls his own destiny, Transcendentalism, the rebellious child of orthodox Unitarianism, intensified this tendency, in fact climaxed it, by arguing that God is immanent in man."[167]

Two representative essays elucidate Emerson's thought.

Nature (from *Essays, Second Series*, 1844)

In 1833 Emerson had traveled to Italy, France, and England, where he, like Channing a decade before him, met Wordsworth and Coleridge. Three years later, he anonymously published *Nature*. While Emerson

---

164 Noll, *A History of Christianity in the United States*, 186.
165 David Lyttle, *Studies in Religion in Early American Literature* (Lanham, MD: University Press of America, 1983), 126.
166 Joel Porte and Saundra Morris, *The Cambridge Companion to Ralph Waldo Emerson* (Cambridge: Cambridge University Press, 1999), 98.
167 Lyttle, *Studies in Religion in Early American Literature*, 94-5.

was more influenced by Coleridge, his essay glimmered with reflections of Wordsworth's nature worship, calling for "an original relation to the universe."[168]

A decade later, Emerson produced another essay entitled "Nature"; by this time, he had moved beyond Unitarianism. This essay expounds his reverence for nature:

> There are days which occur in this climate, at almost any season of the year, wherein the world reaches its perfection, when the air, the heavenly bodies, and the earth, make a harmony, as if nature would indulge her offspring . . . when everything that has life gives sign of satisfaction, and the cattle that lie on the ground seem to have great and tranquil thoughts. . . . At the gates of the forest, the surprised man of the world is forced to leave his city estimates of great and small, wise and foolish. The knapsack of custom falls off his back with the first step he makes into these precincts. Here is sanctity which shames our religions . . . Here we find nature to be the circumstance which dwarfs every other circumstance, and judges like a god all men that come to her.[169]

In this inviting scene, the essay makes a connection between beauty and pleasure, pulsating with words such as perfection, harmony, happiest, pure, sanctity. He summarizes, "Beauty breaks in everywhere" (238). Emerson sets idyllic nature in contrast to society: "Here no history, or church, or state, is interpolated on the divine sky and the immortal year" (236).

He proceeds to speak of how evolutionary geology has shown not only the "secularity of nature," but also "how inconceivably remote is man!" (240) In the face of overwhelming odds, man must realize his own greatness. If we are going to accomplish anything, we must think big.

With statements such as "we feel the soul of the workman streams through us" (246), Emerson moved beyond Channing, who opposed any philosophy that tended to dissolve individual personhood. He also went beyond the English Romanticism of Wordsworth and Coleridge. As a center to life, nature was unable to hold them, and both of them returned to Trinitarian Christianity. Emerson never even went back to Unitarianism.

Fate (from *The Conduct of Life*, 1860)

Between 1851 and 1861, Emerson traveled to western New York to lecture. During the Second Great Awakening, this area had been the scene of many religious revivals, including those conducted by the evangelist Charles Grandison Finney (1792-1875), who "may have had a greater impact on the public life of antebellum America than any of the

---

168   Ralph Waldo Emerson, *Nature*, ed. Joseph L. Blau (Liberal Arts Press, 1948), 1.
169   Ralph Waldo Emerson, "Nature," (from *Essays, Second* Series, 1844), Ralph *Waldo Emerson*, ed. Richard Poirier (New York and Oxford: Oxford University Press, 1990), 235. Subsequent references to this text are given in parentheses.

nation's politicians."[170] From 1825 to 1831, Finney carried on revivals in towns along the Erie Canal, reaching the height of his career in Rochester, at the time the fastest growing city in the United States.[171]

Because of the frequent revivals in western New York, Finney called it the "burned-over district." He explained, "There had been a wild excitement passing through . . . which they called a revival of religion, but which turned out to be spurious."[172] The path between New England and western New York during the early 1800s has been called a "psychic highway," as it nurtured such movements as Shakerism, Mormonism, spiritualism (Rochester "rappings" of 1848), abolitionism (Frederick Douglass lived in Rochester), perfectionism, women's rights (Seneca Falls), and the sexual communism of the Oneida community. Mesmerism, phrenology, Millerism (now Seventh Day Adventism), and Swedenborgianism also found a home there. Finney traveled this route, and he became the founder of modern high-pressure evangelism: "Are you interested in the blood of Jesus Christ? If not, repent, *repent now*, of all your wickedness, and lay hold on the hope that is set before you."[173]

Unlike many others of the time, Emerson did not find Finney's preaching irresistible. Emerson was unimpressed with Finney's "extolling God's heart at the expense of his head."[174]

Emerson's essay "Fate" typified the kind of message that he would bring along the psychic highway to the burned-over district. Significantly, Emerson opens the essay with a discussion of "the Spirit of the Times."[175] He urges that people take up the big challenges. For Emerson, nothing loomed larger than the opposition between polarities.

On the one hand, "there is Fate, or laws of the world" (346). Citing "science," Emerson speaks of the limitations of power, "Nature is what you may do . . . The book of nature is the book of Fate" (350-1). Races arise, and "when a race has lived its term, it comes no more again" (351). Although people may seem powerless before Fate, there is another side. That is the other great force—"power, which is the other fact in the dual world, immense" (354). Power includes intellect and freedom. Emerson asserts that "a part of Fate is the freedom of man" (354).

While the weak use Fate as an excuse, the strong see it as their Destiny. Paradoxically, Fate teaches courage, and "man can confront fate with fate" (355). As in "Nature," Emerson saw the beautiful, so

---

170 Noll, *A History of Christianity in the United States*, 170.
171 Gordon S. Wood, "Evangelical America and Early Mormonism," *New York History. Quarterly Journal of New York State Historical Association*. vol. 61, No. 4 (October 1980), p. 360.
172 Noll, *Eerdmans' Handbook to Christianity in* America, 174.
173 Charles G. Finney, "Stewardship," in *25 of the Greatest Sermons Ever Preached*, ed. Jerry Falwell (Grand Rapids: Baker, 1983), 72.
174 Quoted in See Sallee Fox Engstrom, *The Infinitude of the Private Man: Emerson's Presence in Western New York, 1851 – 1861* (New York: Peter Lang, 1997), 39.
175 Ralph Waldo Emerson, "Fate," (from *Essays, Second* Series, 1844), *Ralph Waldo Emerson*, ed. Richard Poirier, 345. Subsequent references to this text are given in parentheses.

in Fate he sees the positive: "A breath of will blows eternally through the universe of souls in the direction of the right and Necessary" (356). But knowledge is not enough. There must be will: "The one serious and formidable thing in nature is a will" (357).

Here Emerson moves to a higher level. He climbs one last rung and sings a paean to monism (all is one): "Let us build altars to the Blessed Unity which holds nature and souls in perfect solution, and compels every atom to serve an universal end (365). In concluding "Fate," as in "Nature," Emerson has used his reason, but he has traveled the road of emotions and the will.

Emerson's transcendental thought was to influence friends and understudies, such as Henry David Thoreau and Walt Whitman (with his "pagan-pantheist rejoicing in creation"[176]). Although for Emerson, "the calamity is the masses,"[177] he was to have far-reaching impact.

So close in time and space and yet so distant from the faith of a Finney, Emerson's essays were nonetheless charged with the Romantic emotionalism of the times. His paeans to Nature and Fate are at points hauntingly reminiscent—while falling short—of songs such as that of New Englanders Ray Palmer (1808-87) and Lowell Mason (1792-1872); their hymn "My Faith Looks Up to Thee" ends with poignant words of faith in Christ:

> When ends life's transient dream,
>
> When death's cold, sullen stream Shall o'er me roll,
>
> Blest Savior, then, in love, Fear and distrust remove;
>
> Oh, bear me safe above, A ransomed soul![178]

AMERICAN ROMANTICISM: EDGAR ALLAN POE

More than a century and a half after his death, Edgar Allan Poe (1809-49) remains surrounded by mystery and uncertainty. Not infrequently, the contrast between Emerson and him is not favorable to Poe. Indeed, much of Poe's work is dark, and his life was tumultuous. It was beset by death (his mother, foster mother, and young wife), addiction to alcohol and experimentation with drugs, rejection, poverty (he sold the poem "The Raven" for no more than $15), and frustration. Although Emerson was never personally attacked by Poe's stinging criticism, he shared the New England disdain for Poe. Yet in the short lifetime, Poe managed to invent almost single handedly the horror story, detective story, and science fiction.[179]

---

176 Marty, *Righteous Empire*, 117.
177 Alfred Kazin, *God and the American Writer* (New York Knopf, 1997), 49.
178 Palmer wrote the words and Mason the melody of this hymn. "My Faith Looks Up to Thee," hymn 402 in *Christian Worship*.
179 See Jeffrey Meyers, *Edgar Allan Poe: His Life and Legacy* (New York: Scribner's, 1992), 280.

Poe was far removed from the staid and religiously rich and heavy New England background of Emerson. During his brief stay at the University of Virginia, Poe encountered none of the religious tradition that met Emerson at Harvard. The school was only a year old when Poe matriculated in February 1826. Thomas Jefferson was the school's first head. In this Neo-Classical setting, there was no chair of theology, no church on campus, and no required attendance at chapel. On Sundays, Jefferson invited students to dine with him at Monticello; and it's likely that Poe would have met Jefferson before he died on July 4, 1826.

Even earlier, Poe had had other experiences that set him outside ordinary American culture. In July 1815, a mere six months after war between America and Britain ended, his foster father John Allan took the family to his native England. Such exposure was bound to make him keenly aware of the Age of Reason scene.

Yet in most of his life and art, Poe would come to epitomize the Romantic and modern dilemma of insecurity and fragmentation. In Poe we find the mind struggling to find a sense of certainty. This thread runs through Romantic literature and is especially evident in Poe's work. Three characteristic short stories along with Poe's statement of personal belief indicate his thought in relation to the spiritual and philosophical ideas of antebellum America.

A Descent into the Maelström (1841)

This story tells of a Norwegian fisherman's experience of being drawn into the dreadful Moskoe-ström, a whirlpool that periodically develops and recedes. Poe's attitude toward *nature* is evident—not that of beauty observed in serenity and recalled in joyful reflection (ala Wordsworth's *Tintern Abbey*). It is nature in its awesome sublimity. Early in the story the narrator joins the old fisherman in viewing the Maelström from high atop a cliff. Poe's description of nature could not differ more from that of Emerson.

> I looked dizzily, and beheld a wide expanse of ocean whose waters were so inky a hue as to bring at once to my mind the Nubian geographer's account of the *Mare Tenebrarum*. A panorama more deplorably desolate no human imagination can conceive. To the right and left, as far as the eye could reach, there lay outstretched, like ramparts of the world, lines of horridly black and beetling cliff, whose character of gloom was but the more forcibly illustrated by the surf which reared high up against it its white and ghastly crest, howling and shrieking for ever.[180]

Poe proceeds to describe the Maelström in terms of the American symbol of sublimity, Niagara Falls (137). The fisherman relates how he and

---

180 Edgar Allan Poe, "A Descent into the Maelström," *The Portable Poe,* ed. Philip Van Doren Stern (New York: Penguin, 1973), 135. Subsequent references to this text are given in parentheses.

his two brothers were in their boat when a hurricane drew them into the whirlpool. One brother was swept overboard and killed. As the two remaining brothers wildly circled the vortex, the survivor observed that cylindrical objects were the least likely to be destroyed. Lashing himself to a cask, he jumped into the water and watched as his older brother was drawn into the depths and destroyed with their boat.

Poe makes some religious allusions in the story. As the sailor tells of his experience, he says, "I muttered a hurried prayer to God, and thought all was over" (148). No content to the prayer is mentioned, nor is any hope of heaven. While the fisherman whirls downward toward what seems to be certain death, he says, "I began to reflect how magnificent a thing it was to die in such a manner, and how foolish it was in me to think of so paltry a consideration as my own individual life, in view of so wonderful a manifestation of God's power" (147). What Poe's sailor refers to as God could just as well be Nature or Fate, since there is nothing personal about this God.

As Emerson had called on man to use his powers of intellect in the face of Fate, so the sailor did just that. Noting how cylindrical objects stayed higher in the whirlpool, he saw his chance. Thomas Jefferson would have been pleased with such behavior, in light of his talk of "habits of reflection and correct action." But Poe was going beyond that, as he anticipated both the horrors of the modern world and the isolation of the individual, who can only survive by the use of his rationality. In its use of reason and its description of the sublime, the story harks back to the Enlightenment. In its suspension of belief and its uncertainty, it is Romantic.

The Black Cat (1843)

Just as Poe differed from Emerson in his view of nature, he also differed concerning *human nature*. Poe, and Baudelaire after him, rejected the idea of innate goodness.[181] "The Black Cat" was Poe's first story to deal with his theme of the "perverse."

In this story, a condemned murderer gives the account of his crime. He begins, "[T]omorrow I die, and to-day I would unburthen my soul."[182] The protagonist-narrator, like Poe himself, is an alcoholic. He and his wife owned a pet black cat, whose name was Pluto (no doubt after the god of the underworld). In a drunken rage, the owner had gouged out one of the cat's eyes.

Later, in another rage, he took the cat into the yard, hanged it by its neck, and declared that he "hung it *because* I knew that in so doing I was committing a sin—a deadly sin that would so jeopardize my immortal

---

181 Charles Baudelaire, *Baudelaire on Poe*, trans. and ed. Lois and Francis E. Hyslop, Jr. (State College, PA: Bald Eagle Press, 1952), 22.
182 Poe, "The Black Cat," *The Portable Poe*, 296. Subsequent references to this text are given in parentheses.

soul as to place it—if such a thing were possible—even beyond the reach of the Most Merciful and Most Terrible God" (300). That same night, the man's house burned down, except for newly plastered wall that strangely bore the image of the cat and noose.

Later, he brought home another one-eyed cat—also black, except for a white mark resembling a gallows. The new cat now begins to irritate him. He uses Biblical terminology as he describes his hatred for this cat: "And *a brute beast* . . . —*a brute beast* to work out for *me*—for me a man, fashioned in the image of the High God" (304). One day he tries to kill the cat with an axe, and when his wife tries to prevent him, he kills her. "[I] buried the axe in her brain" (305).

He places her body in a basement alcove and plastered it over. When police come to search the house they find nothing. Proud of his successfully concealed crime, the man taps with his cane on the wall, from which comes a shriek. The narrator's self-satisfaction changes as he exclaims: "But may God shield me and deliver me from the fangs of the Arch-Fiend! . . . I was answered by a voice from within the tomb! . . . a howl—a wailing shriek, half of horror and half of triumph, . . . I had walled the monster up within the tomb!" (308) Inside the wall the police find the corpse with the black cat on its head.

The Imp of the Perverse (1845)

This is another story about a condemned murderer who tells his account. After years of concealing his crime, the criminal is driven by an uncontrollable "perverse" impulse to turn himself in and confess. Poe was well aware of contemporary movements as, for example, mesmerism and phrenology. In the opening paragraph of "The Imp of the Perverse," Poe's protagonist speaks of "phrenologists," as we might refer to psychologists, people who study human thought, emotions, and behavior. He says that they, together with others who are afflicted with the "arrogance of reason," have set aside "faith—whether it be faith in Revelation, or faith in the Kabbala."[183] In "The Imp of the Perverse," Poe is torn between a natural and supernatural explanation for unexplainable behavior.

The narrator describes how he planned and carried out a murder by using a poisoned candle. The murderer inherits the estate and lives happily, and without pangs of conscience, until . . . One day, he is driven by the imp to confess. He does so and consigns himself "to the hangman and to hell" (1226). The reference to hell is merely a figure of speech. The narrator's final words express his attitude about the life to come: "Today

---
183 Edgar Allan Poe, "The Imp of the Perverse," *Collected Works of Edgar Allan Poe*, ed. Thomas Ollive Mabbot (Cambridge, MA and London: Belknap Press of Harvard University Press, 1978), 1219. Subsequent references to this text are given in parentheses.

I wear these chains, and am *here*! To-morrow I shall be fetterless!—*but where?*" (1226) Like life in this world, that to come is uncertain.

Eureka (1848)

Poe held to neither the Trinitarian nor Unitarian faith. Moreover, he rejected America's "naïve faith in the omnipotence of industry . . . [the] national mania of materialism."[184] Toward the end of his life, Poe published *Eureka*, his statement of man's relationship to the universe and God. "Poe, the archrationalist, had frequently criticized the Transcendentalists for their lack of intellectual rigor and called them 'mystics for mysticism's sake,'" writes one biographer, "But in *Eureka* he became more mystical than any of them . . . Filled with erroneous 'facts' and fantastic speculations, the book has no scientific merit . . . confused by the contents of his own mind, Poe could not—as Byron said of Coleridge—explain his own explanations."[185]

The book says, for example, that "each soul is, in part, its own God—its own Creator:—in a word, that God—the material *and* spiritual God—*now* exists solely in the diffused Matter and Spirit of the Universe."[186] Poe further declares, "Unity . . . is a truth—I feel it. Diffusion is a truth—I see it."[187] Governed by irrational forces and surrounded by a terrifying natural world, man can only look ahead to death, without a Savior or hope of any sort of direct union with God.

Such alienation has struck responsive chords. "As a poet, Edgar Allan Poe is a man apart," wrote Charles Baudelaire, who translated his works into French; "Almost by himself he represents the romantic movement on the other side of the Atlantic."[188] Although his genius is respected more in Europe than in his native America, his influence has been acknowledged on both sides of the Atlantic. Poe's employer George Graham said, "Literature to him was religion; and he, its high-priest."[189]

Emerson and Poe

Ralph Waldo Emerson and Edgar Allan Poe were contemporaries, sharing the Romantic transition from reason to intuition, from social conformity to individual creativity. Both drew heavily on European sources. Both were relatively unaffected by the popular Protestant Christianity of the day, and both shunned the fringe movements of antebellum America. Both understood the nakedness of the human condition in the face of nature.

---

184 Lois and Francis E. Hyslop, "Introduction," Baudelaire, *Baudelaire on Poe*, 22.
185 Meyers, *Edgar Allan Poe: His Life and Legacy*, 214.
186 Poe, *Eureka*, in *The Portable Poe*, 662.
187 As quoted in Lyttle, *Studies in Religion in Early American Literature*, 33.
188 Baudelaire, *Baudelaire on Poe*, 67.
189 Meyers, *Edgar Allan Poe: His Life and Legacy*, 282.

In other ways, they were far apart. Emerson became the optimistic spokesman of Nature and Fate. We see him kneeling at the altar of Blessed Unity and Beautiful Necessity. A century after his death, we see him arise as Transcendental forerunner of the New Age.

As for Poe—in retrospect as in life, he remains the symbol of the individual struggling against the Maelströms without and the Perverse within. He built no altars, yet for many he remains High Priest, holding the censer while the smoke ascends into the darkness.

PART 4
THE VICTORIAN AGE: 1850—1900

CHARLES DICKENS: MAN IN THE MIDDLE

"What remains standing in Europe?" lamented Tsar Nicolas I to Queen Victoria in 1848, when revolutions were rocking Europe. The tsar went on to answer his own question, "Great Britain and Russia."[190] It seemed that Victorian England was an island of security in a world of upheaval and political instability. Queen Victoria, whose "self-contentment and sense of moral respectability reflected the attitudes of her time,"[191] had the longest reign in English history, from 1837 to 1901. Such was her impact that the era in which she lived is known as the Victorian Age.

Charles Dickens—Quintessential Victorian

Charles Dickens (1812-70) was the most celebrated Victorian writer and to this day remains "the most popular and internationally known of English novelists."[192] Among novelists of all ages, he is a monumental artist. A token indication of his ongoing influence is that more than *ninety* films have been based on the works of Dickens.[193] While other Romantic and Victorian writers represent a transition into new religious thought, Dickens seems to represent the passing of the old. He espoused an anthropocentric worldview yet also held to elements of the old.

Dickens and the Victorian Milieu

Even while the late Romantic poets Keats, Shelley, and Byron were trying to forge a worldview outside the traditional Christian framework, nineteenth century England remained a predominately Christian land: "During [Queen Victoria's] long reign both the Church of England and the free churches greatly increased their membership."[194] Indeed, the

---
190 William J. Duiker and Jackson J. Spielvogel. *World History,* vol. 2: *Since 1500,* second edition. (Belmont, CA: West/Wadsworth, 1998, 784.
191 Duiker and Spielvogel, *World History,* vol. 2, 797.
192 Wynne-Davies, *Prentice Hall Guide to English Literature,* 459.
193 "Charles Dickens Filmography," http://us.imdb.com/Name?Dickens,+Charles.
194 Roberts and Roberts, *A History of England,* vol. 2, 616.

free, Nonconformist churches experienced spectacular growth during the period, growing in membership from less than one million to more than two million.

In spite of outward growth, not all was well with English Christianity. One of the most profound changes was the erosion of age-old religious beliefs in the face of scientific writings. More than that, English Christianity had fragmented into a wide array of beliefs and sects.

Dickens' parents were Anglican, apparently "uninterested in dogma" and "probably not very regular in their worship."[195] Years later, in a letter, Dickens expressed his dislike for the doctrinal divisions of the Christian churches: "The spectacle presented by the indecent squabbles of priests of most denominations, and the exemplary unfairness and rancour with which they conduct their differences, utterly repel me."[196] Nevertheless, his mother "dragged" the young Dickens to hear a powerful preacher.[197] The seeds were sown for a lifelong antipathy toward this type of religion.

The London of Charles Dickens was also the home of the Baptist minister Charles Haddon Spurgeon (1834-92), known as the "prince of preachers" and perhaps the greatest preacher in English history. At the age of twenty-one, Spurgeon became the pastor of the New Park Chapel in London, a small congregation of perhaps a hundred people. Within a short time, he was the most popular preacher in the world, preaching to weekly crowds of over 10,000. During his ministry, Spurgeon's sermons were distributed worldwide and read weekly by millions. Over 3500 of them are still in print and read by more people than any other preacher in history.[198]

Spurgeon's evangelistic brand of Christianity was hardly to Dickens' taste. Yet, according to his children, Dickens was a dedicated Christian. Henry Fielding Dickens wrote of his father: "His religious convictions, though he never made a parade of them, were very strong and deep ... So strong was this feeling, indeed, that he wrote the simple history of Our Lord's life for us when we were children."[199]

During Dickens' lifetime, while Christianity was growing in middle class society, belief among society's upper and lower economic and educational strata was unraveling:

> The majority of the working classes attended no church and had little faith, the result of poverty, ignorance, and neglect, not skeptical reason. Skeptical reason ... [made] inroads into the educated classes. An expanding, all encroaching rationalism had produced a

---

[195] Paul Schlicke, ed., *Oxford Reader's Companion to Dickens* (New York: Oxford University Press, 1999), 492.
[196] Raymond L. Brett, *Faith and Doubt: Religion and Secularization in Literature from Wordsworth to Larkin* (Cambridge: James Clarke, 1997), 124.
[197] Dennis Walder, *Dickens and Religion* (London: George Allen and Unwin, 1981), 7.
[198] See, for example, Roberts and Roberts, *A History of England*, vol. 2, 616.
[199] Henry Fielding Dickens, *Memories of My Father* (London: Victor Gollancz, 1928), 28-9.

self conscious, earnest, aggressive agnosticism. The expansion of population, literacy, and knowledge allowed a parallel advance of both religion and doubt, belief and unbelief.[200]

Dickens personally experienced both the poverty and wealth of the first nation to achieve the Industrial Revolution. He knew firsthand and recorded the struggles of people living in the slums as well as in the mansions of the world's greatest metropolis, London.

Machines and the laws of nature appeared to join forces in reducing all existence to what worked and what furthered material progress. Utilitarianism, or Benthamism, became the philosophy of the day, paralleling the rise of evangelical religion. In what were thought to be fixed economic laws, the poor were considered a part of nature, not to be encouraged by charity, but to be forced into workhouses. According to Thomas Malthus, charity only encouraged their animal-like fertility.[201] With less people, there would be more wealth for those who deserved it. Espousing "the greatest happiness for the greatest number," Benthamism advocated self-interest, the achievement of pleasure and the avoidance of pain.

The writers Carlyle, Ruskin, and Dickens were "the most eloquent and implacable literary foes of Utilitarianism."[202] To political economists, however, man "was nothing more than an economic unit, a contributory digit to a statistical total . . . Benthamism offended all decent sympathies, those springing from Christian morality and, more immediately, from the romantic spirit."[203] A review of Dickens' two first-person novels illuminates his approach to religion.

David Copperfield

The final installments of *David Copperfield* were published in 1850. That same mid-century year marked the return of the Roman Catholic hierarchy to England, and a year later, another Charles, the young Charles Haddon Spurgeon, would preach his first sermon at the age of seventeen. *David Copperfield* was Dickens' eighth novel, and many consider it his greatest. In many ways, the book is autobiographical.

In combing through Dickens' works, James S. Stevens came up with a total of almost 250 Biblical allusions.[204] Given the vast number of pages in Dickens' works, allusions to the Scriptures are relatively few and far between. Yet there are enough to indicate that Dickens is working within a culture still relatively conversant with the Bible. *David Copperfield,* contains fifteen references to the Bible, not many for an 800-page book.

---
200   Roberts and Roberts, *A History of England*, vol. 2, 616-7.
201   Richard D. Altick, *Victorian People and Ideas* (New York: Norton, 1973), 124.
202   Altick, *Victorian People and Ideas,* 137.
203   Altick, *Victorian People and Ideas,* 137.
204   James S. Stevens, "Dickens' Use of the English Bible," *The Dickensian,* 21 (1925): 218.

Dickens was an advocate of that approach to religion which came to be known as the "social gospel." According to this movement, regardless of one's doctrinal inclinations, the priority for any Christian is to help the needy. This concern for social action brought him into conflict with Utilitarianism. For Dickens, the simple yet heroic Ham, who loses his life trying to save others in a storm, is a noble portrait of self-sacrifice as opposed to mere self-satisfaction.

His antipathy to Utilitarianism did not make Dickens a friend of conservative, Bible-believing, evangelical Christianity. In *David Copperfield*, the evil Mr. John Murdstone and his sister represent such religiosity. David says of them, "Firmness, I may observe, was the grand quality on which both Mr. And Miss Murdstone took their stand . . . it was another name for tyranny." [205] Spurgeon, known as the outstanding heir of the Puritans, "much disliked the anti-Evangelical bias" of Dickens.[206]

While the Bible certainly speaks of helping the needy and of applying oneself, it ultimately places all of life under the umbrella of God's providence. In the words of the psalmist David, "But I trust in you, O Lord . . . My times are in your hands" (Psalm 31:15). This concept is not entirely missing in *David Copperfield*. It falls to Agnes to expound it, as she advises David, "There is God to trust in!" (535) At novel's close, Agnes is David's everything. Human love becomes the center and lodestar of life.

At times, Dickens' focus in *David Copperfield* does move beyond the earthbound needs of people. Twice in *David Copperfield*, he refers to John 11, the story of the raising of Lazarus from the dead, including Jesus' statement, "I am the resurrection and the life," words used for the funeral service in *The Book of Common Prayer*.

Great Expectations

In 1857, a record crowd of 23,654 came to hear Spurgeon preach at London's Crystal Palace. In 1861, the 6,000 seat Metropolitan Tabernacle was built for Spurgeon and packed twice each Sunday to hear him preach. That same year, John Stuart Mills's *Utilitarianism* appeared; and Charles Dickens completed *Great Expectations*.

During the middle years of Dickens' adult life, he had moved toward Unitarianism, but later returned to Anglicanism, generally reserving his approval of clergymen who were "worldly, urbane and cultured latitudinarians."[207] *Great Expectations* was conceived and written during a period of deep personal reflection and soul-searching.

---

205 Charles Dickens, *David Copperfield* (London: Penguin Books, 1996), 54. Subsequent references to this work are given in parentheses.
206 Ernest W. Bacon, *Spurgeon: Heir of the Puritans* (Grand Rapids: Baker, 1967), 109.
207 Walder, *Dickens and Religon*, 210.

Great Expectations has even less Biblical terminology than Dickens' other works, with only three references. Two of them are superficial; the third is not. As Abel Magwich lies on his deathbed, the protagonist Pip reads the Bible to him. When Magwich dies, Pip says, "Mindful, then, of what we had read together, I thought of the two men who went up to the Temple to pray, and I knew there were no better words that I could say beside his bed, than 'O Lord, be merciful to him a sinner!'" [208] The reference is to Luke 18:9-14, the story of the Pharisee and the tax collector, which Jesus told "to some who were confident of their own righteousness and looked down on everybody else." In the Bible, the words "God, be merciful to me, a sinner" belong to the humble tax collector, who is "justified before God," while the proud Pharisee is not.

For Dickens, humanity's first concern is not getting right with God, but getting right with one's fellowman. Dickens "rejected Original sin. In fact, 'sin' is scarcely mentioned at all," and the "more mysterious doctrines of Redemption and Grace concerned [Dickens] very little, the technique of worship not at all. . . . His religion is emphatically one of works, not faith." [209]

This was hardly the view of historic Christianity, which focuses on *the* great sacrifice of God's Son for the fallen human race. Spurgeon put it this way, "Oh the numbers of books that have been written to prove that the cross means an example of self-sacrifice; as if every martyrdom did not mean that. They cannot endure a real substitutionary sacrifice for human guilt, and an effectual purgation of sin by the death of the great substitute. Yet the cross means that or nothing." [210] This was not to say that because Christ has won salvation the Christian could expect a life of ease. In another sermon, Spurgeon declared, "When you begin to serve God, and for His sake endeavour to benefit your fellow mortals, do not expect any reward from men, except to be misunderstood, suspected, and abused. . . . Who seeks for ease when he has seen the Lord Christ? If Christ wears a crown of thorns, shall we covet a crown of laurel?" [211]

Even though Dickens' religion was the most general type, he was not ready to take the step into a Christ-less and Scripture-less religion. Dickens wrote to his son:

> I most strongly and affectionately impress upon you the priceless value of the New Testament, and the study of that book as the one unfailing guide in life. Deeply respecting it and bowing down before the characters of our Saviour, as separated from the vain constructions and conventions of men, you cannot go very wrong . . . [212]

---
208 Charles Dickens, *Great Expectations* (London: Penguin Books, 1996), 460.
209 Humphrey House, *The Dickens World* (London and New York: Oxford University Press, 1950), 111-2.
210 Charles H. Spurgeon, *Twelve Sermons on the Passion and Death of Christ* (Grand Rapids: Baker, 1971), 146.
211 Spurgeon, *Twelve Sermons on the Passion and Death of Christ*, 100-1.
212 Stevens, "Dickens' Use of the English Bible," 32.

In his later novels Dickens seemed to move almost irresistibly closer to historic Christianity's teaching of original sin. More and more, he came to see the depth of human wickedness.

Dickens and His Audience

Dickens' work was bound to elicit a mixed reaction. As much as he kept clear of explicit religious opinions in his writing, people picked up on what he wrote:

> In his own time Dickens could not have failed to notice the impact of his beliefs—or supposed lack of them—upon committed readers, ecstatically welcomed as he was by liberal Christians, especially in America, and reviled by the more evangelical wing of the faith. . . . by the time of his death in 1870 "eulogies, almost idolatrous" could be heard, "every Unitarian and Universalist pulpit" in Boston sending him "to heaven immediately". . . Other allegiances led to remarks of a different kind: the High Church *Christian Remembrancer* . . . found "mere pagan seritinientalism" in his pages; the *Dublin Review* . . . accused him of "libel" against the Catholic religion, and concluded after his death that his works were "as false as any of those of the undisguisedly materialistic writers of the day" . . .[213]

Dickens simply wanted to hold to a childlike faith in a loving God. Yet the history of the Christian church is one of constant struggle, of "contending for the faith" (Jude 3), with others within the pale of the church and with those who would challenge it from outside. For Christianity is not merely a faith that believes, but a faith that believes in something. Moreover, there have been individuals who have been able to enter the fields of polemics and apologetics as the Bible urges, "with gentleness and respect" (1 Peter 3:15).

Dickens was a child of his times. He still held to a belief in the life to come, and he was not ashamed to call Christ his Savior. In this, Dickens was clinging to a faith that would eventually lose its grip on the masses for whom he wrote. Charles Dickens was a man in the middle.

> *"I commit my soul to the mercy of God through our Lord and Saviour Jesus Christ."*
>
> (From the last will and testament of Charles John Huffam Dickens, May 12, 1869)[214]

ALFRED LORD TENNYSON AND THE SPIRIT OF THE AGE

During Victoria's reign, England reached its greatest heights of power, wealth, and influence, but that stability was superficial. The Vic-

---

213 Walder, *Dickens and Religion*, 5.
214 Stephen Rost, "The Faith behind the Famous," *Christian History*, 9:3 (1990): 41.

torian period was anything but stable. It was, as one compendium notes, "the age when change rather than stability came first to be accepted as normal in the nature of human outlook. . . ."[215] Just when religion was struggling with scientific and philosophical challenges, two new opponents appeared on the horizon.

One was higher criticism, which reduced the Bible to another piece of literature to be studied in light of its historical setting, rather than as an inerrant revelation from above. In 1846, George Eliot translated from the German David Strauss's *Life of Jesus,* which posited Christ as a historical figure and not a divine being. The other antagonist had emerged a decade earlier: Charles Lyell's *Principles of Geology* (1830-33) appeared on the scene confronting long-held beliefs about a relatively young age for the earth. The work struck at two historic theological tenets— belief in the special, six-day creation and the worldwide Flood.

It did not take long for intellectuals to apply the concept beyond the geological realm:

> [T]o move from the Romantic to the Victorian period is, with many exceptions and qualifications, to move from catastrophism to literary uniformitarianism. . . . Beginning as a catastrophist under the shadow of Milton and the great Romantics, [Tennyson] moved in his middle years toward uniformitarianism but then, as darkness settled over his vision, moved back toward catastrophism again.[216]

England was ripe for the acceptance of new doctrines of major import. The 1851 religious census in England showed that out of a population of 17,927,609, only 7,261,032 "attended some kind of service on the census Sunday."[217]

Tennyson and the Occult

This was the England in which Alfred Lord Tennyson lived. His life (1809-92), like that of his queen, spans an era and symbolizes a nation, an empire, and an age. Tennyson was the great successor to the Romantics, and he went on to succeed Wordsworth as Poet Laureate.

Tennyson was not only a product of the movements of the times. He was also a product of the immediate environment of his family and friends. He was born at Somersby, Lincolnshire, the fourth of twelve children of the Reverend George Clayton Tennyson and his wife Elizabeth. Clayton was given to "outbursts of temper, abusive language, heavy drinking, and . . . addiction to laudanum and other drugs." [218] Much of Tennyson's life was devoted to the pursuit of personal stability. His adult life was also shaped by Arthur Hallam, an intimate friend he

---
215 Wynne-Davis, *Prentice Hall Guide to English Literature,* 996.
216 A Dwight Culler, *The Poetry of Tennyson* (New Haven and London: Yale University Press, 1977), 15.
217 Sanders, *The Short Oxford History of English Literature,* 399.
218 Norman Page, *Tennyson: An Illustrated Life* (New York: New Amersterdam Books, 1993), 34.

met at Cambridge. It was Hallam's death that served as the catalyst for *In Memoriam*, the poem which, perhaps more than any other work, gave voice to the spirit of the times.

Tennyson's life exhibited a steady movement away from historic Christianity toward occultism. By the end of the nineteenth century, occult societies had become the vogue among many intellectuals. Occultist A. P. Sinnet asserts, Tennyson was an occultist ahead of his time:

> [Tennyson] was the reincarnation of an Ego that had in previous centuries been manifesting as a great poet over and over again. Advanced occultists know now that in successive lives he was Virgil, Omar Khayyam, Dante and Spenser before he culminated as a greater than any of these—Tennyson.[219]

We share neither Sinnett's belief in reincarnation nor his contention that Tennyson was "a greater than any of these"; he was not above the others as story teller or epic poet. Nevertheless, Tennyson did recount a type of extra-sensory experience, which he described as "a kind of walking trance I have frequently had. . . . individuality itself seemed to dissolve and fade away . . . the loss of personality being no extinction but the only true life."[220]

Tennyson had more than a passing interest in the paranormal. Here seemed to be a way to harmonize the new evolutionary ideas with a personal spirituality. Later in life, in 1882, Tennyson became a founding member of the Society for Psychical Research.[221] Over the years his poetry moved away from a direct use of the Bible to more abstraction, until the Scriptures became little more than a literary tool.[222] Yet atheism appalled him, and he said, "People must have some religion."[223]

In Memoriam

In Memoriam reflects both the thoughts of its author and the spirit of the age. *In Memoriam* was inspired by the untimely death of Hallam in 1833. Tennyson wrote the lengthy poem over sixteen years (finishing it five years before his famous "Charge of the Light Brigade"). By the time *In Memoriam* was completed, the figure of Hallam had given way to an abstraction.

The poem opens with a prologue that addresses Christ, the "Son of God."[224] No doubt this explains why most readers received it [as a]

---

219   A. P. Sinnett, *Tennyson an Occultist: As His Writings Prove* (1920; reprint, Haskell House Publisher: New York: 1972), 12.
220   As quoted in Culler, *The Poetry of Tennyson*, 1.
221   See, for example, Page, *Tennyson, An Illustrated Life*, 149.
222   See Edna Moore Robinson, *Tennyson's Use of the Bible* (Baltimore: Johns Hopkins Press, 1917).
223   Page, *Tennyson, An Illustrated Life*, 150.
224   Alfred Tennyson, *Tennyson's Poetry: Authoritative Texts, Juvenilia and Early Responses, Criticism*, ed. Robert W. Hill, Jr. (New York and London: W. W. Norton, 1971), 119. Subsequent quotes from the poem are from this edition.

homely Christian elegy."²²⁵ Yet the prologue was not written until 1848 and appears as a paste-on to the body of the poem. *In Memoriam* begins:

> I held it truth, with him who sings
>
> To one clear harp in divers tones,
>
> That men may rise on stepping-stones
>
> Of their dead selves to higher things.

Here the poet begins his struggles to build something new. Initially, Tennyson seems certain of the immortality of the soul and that he will see Hallam again. The theme of immortality reflects the Bible and specifically the account of the raising of Lazarus in John 11. But no sooner does he recount that story than doubts arise. Throughout the poem, Tennyson attempts by various means to attain some sort of assurance concerning immortality.

Ever looming above any hopes of personal immortality is the coldness of nature:

> Who trusted God was love indeed
>
> And love Creation's final law—
>
> Tho' Nature red in tooth and claw
>
> With ravine, shriek'd against his creed— (section 56)

Hope for something beyond the grave must lie in a leap of faith. Communication with the spirit of the deceased comes from one's own spirit being at peace:

> In vain shalt thou, or any call
>
> The spirits from their golden day
>
> Except, like them, thou too canst say,
>
> My spirit is at peace with all. (section 93)

In Memorian expresses Tennyson's adherence to the idea of spiritual evolution to higher and higher types through self-transcendence. In spite of this, the overall mood is less than optimistic:

> There rolls the deep where grew the tree.
>
> O earth what changes hast thou seen!
>
> There, where the long street roars, hath been
>
> The stillness of the central sea. (section 123)

"Such passages," notes Norman Page, "convey a vertiginous sense of solid reality slipping away as unthought-of vistas of time are opened up. It was a sense that Tennyson's was the very first generation to experience."²²⁶ The significance of *In Memoriam* for Tennyson's generation is nicely summarized by Hazelton Spencer:

---

225 Michael Thorn, *Tennyson* (New York: St. Martin's Press, 1992), 243.
226 Page, *Tennyson: An Illustrated Life*, 148.

Tennyson had sloughed off much of Christian theology until his religion was reduced, as it was for many Victorians, to a simple faith in God, in a divine moral law speaking through conscience, and in the immortality of the soul. But the new science of evolution threatened to destroy all religion whatever. What Tennyson did, and what made the poem so significant at the time, was to admit the arguments of "atheistical science" and then answer them by showing that evolution might be given a moral and religious interpretation. . . . Tennyson's answer was not logical but emotional. He simply refused to believe that man was merely a product of nature dying a natural death in a universe of mechanical force.[227]

Within a few months, 60,000 copies of *In Memoriam* were sold. Within twenty years, it went through nineteen editions. Prince Albert's admiration for it was one reason that Tennyson became Poet Laureate. After Albert's death, Queen Victoria told Tennyson, "Next to the Bible, *In Memoriam* is my comfort."[228] Tennyson's struggle to come to terms with the ultimate issues of life and death in a universe that seemed to be growing ever vaster and more impersonal was the struggle of his generation. The intensity of its doubt secures the poem's continued relevance, while the paucity of its faith has kept succeeding generations looking for something more.

CHARLES DARWIN AND THE THEORY OF EVOLUTION

Organic life beneath the shoreless waves

Was born and nurs'd in ocean's pearly caves;

First forms minute, unseen by spheric glass,

Move on the mud, or pierce the watery mass;

These as successive generations bloom,

New powers acquire and larger limbs assume;

Whence countless groups of vegetarian spring,

And breathing realms of fin and feet and wing.[229]

Written by Erasmus Darwin (1731-1802), these lines are from *The Temple of Nature*. Half a century later, Charles Darwin (1809-82) would add to his grandfather's poetic imagination *The Origin of Species*. A great amount of effort has gone into either fortifying or refuting the theory of evolution. Not so much research has been spent on investigating the intellectual milieu that spawned the theory. Of particular interest are the scientific and religious climates of nineteenth century England and how they may have influenced Darwin.

---

227 Hazelton Spencer, Walter E. Houghton and Herbert Barrows, *British Literature: From Blake to the Present Day* (Boston: D. C. Heath, 1952), 635f.
228 George O. Marshall, Jr. *A Tennyson Handbook* (New York: Twayne Publishers, 1963), 122.
229 Quoted in Desmond King-Hele, *Erasmus Darwin* (New York: Charles Scribner's Sons, 1963), 122.

Darwin's Scientific Forerunners

The idea of evolution goes back to the ancients. In the fifth century B. C., Anaxagoras suggested that plants and animals came from pre-existing "germs," while Empedocles suggested that plant life appeared first, and from that came animals, parts of which budded off and came together to form whole animals. A century later, Aristotle proposed the idea of a chain of being, with man at the top. Contrary to Empedocles, Aristotle saw design: "Nature does nothing without an aim. She is always striving after the most beautiful that is possible."[230]

The idea of some sort of evolution was not new. It remained, however, for the eighteenth century to prepare the way for a detailed and full-blown theory. In addition to thinkers such as Kant, a number of scientists set the stage for Darwin to supply the missing link.

In his classifications, Carl Linnaeus (1707-78) used the word "species," the Latin the word for "kind" in the Genesis creation account, a reflection of Linnaeus's deeply held Protestant faith. In Linnaeus's day, the species were considered fixed. Linnaeus based his classifications on similarities in design, regarding each species as bearing the original concept of the Creator.

Comte de Buffon (1707-88) attended a Jesuit college but came to reject the Biblical creation account. Buffon would become Linnaeus's chief critic. He was the first to suggest that species could change with environmental influences and pass those modifications on to their offspring. In *Origin,* Darwin refers to Buffon as "the first author . . . in modern times" to offer a scientific approach to evolution.[231]

Jean-Baptiste Lamarck (1744-1829) worked under Buffon and attended a Jesuit school to become a priest, but lost his faith in the immutability of species and divine creation. He argued that life can begin spontaneously, that animals can pass on acquired characteristics, and that over many generations one species can develop into a new one.

Just as Buffon stood in contrast to Linnaeus, Lamarck had his counterpart in fellow Frenchman Georges Cuvier (1769-1832), a Protestant who reconciled the Biblical record with fossil records and the fixity of the species. According to Cuvier, catastrophes, including the Flood, accounted for the fossil records, while God's providence preserved life on earth.

Unhampered by government censorship, English science took a different tack. The evolutionary theory developed through various individuals, until it emerged full-blown in the works of Charles Darwin. It

---
230   Michael White and John Gribbin, *Darwin: A Life in Science* (New York: Dutton, 1995), 28-30.
231   Charles Darwin, *The Origin of Species* (New York: Mentor, 1958), 17. Subsequent references to this work are indicated with page numbers in parentheses in the text.

seems that many held liberal views of the Bible even before they took up ideas that fed into evolutionary thought.

Thomas Robert Malthus (1766-1834) was influenced by Rousseau, Hume, and the noted Unitarian Joseph Priestley. Sowing the seeds for the doctrine of survival of the fittest, his *Essay on the Principle of Population* (1798) argued that disease, famine, infanticide, and warfare were "legitimate checks on human population and should not be discouraged."[232]

James Hutton (1726-97), a deist, set forth the geological theory of uniformitarianism, contending that currently observable phenomena (e.g., wind, erosion) over long periods of time, rather than geological catastrophes (e.g., the Flood) could account for fossil records.

Charles Lyell (1797-1875) followed Hutton's lead and set out to find evidence to support the theory. Lyell's *Principles of Geology* (1830) held to uniformitarianism. Lyell was troubled by the implications of his ideas, until Darwin persuaded him to think otherwise.

Robert Chambers (1802-71) espoused a theory of evolution, but wanted to keep peace with traditional theology. Claiming the Mosaic account of creation did not give "philosophically exact views of nature," in his *Vestiges of the Natural History of Creation,* Chambers argued that evolution actually exalted God.

Alfred Russel Wallace

Although Alfred Russel Wallace (1823-1913) might be the least recognized name among Darwin's scientific precursors, he is the one man among them who may well lay claim to developing the theory of evolution. His parents were "devout members of the Church of England, but there is little evidence that he had been exposed to the Bible."[233] In fact, he became involved in spiritism and the Society for Psychical Research.

Wallace sailed to the Malay Archipelago and in 1855 published *On the Law Which Has Regulated the Introduction of New Species.* Wallace wrote, "[E]very species had come into existence coincident both in time and space with a pre-existing closely allied species."[234] On reading this, Lyell and Darwin agreed it was a threat to Darwin's being first in the field.

One piece of the puzzle remained unexplained, however. That was why some live while others do not. Again, Wallace found the answer. One night, on the island of Ternate, he recalled Malthus's *Essay*: "There suddenly flashed upon me the idea of the survival of the fittest. The more I thought it over, the more I became convinced that I had at length found

---

232 Ian T. Taylor, *In the Minds of Men: Darwin and the New World Order,* second edition (Toronto: TFE Publishing, 1987), 78.
233 Taylor, *In the Minds of Men,* 74.
234 Taylor, *In the Minds of Men,* 77.

the long-sought-for law of nature that solved the problems of the Origin of Species."[235] Wallace sent a copy of his Ternate paper to Darwin, and a year later Darwin published *On the Origin of Species,* taking the very title from Wallace. For years the standard line had been—and for many it continues to be—that the two men came to their parallel conclusions simultaneously. There is strong circumstantial evidence that Darwin got the key concept of natural selection from Wallace.

Darwin, Science, and Theology

The common understanding of Darwin's relation to the Christian faith is that he clung to it as long as he could, struggling until forced to give it up under the pressure of overwhelming scientific facts. Yet his leanings may have been much less Christian all along. The theological climate of England in Darwin's day was fraught with liberalism. Unitarian faith became more open, organized, and active, with members such as Joseph Priestley in England and Emerson in America. Unitarians rejected the doctrine of the Trinity, miracles, the Flood and Creation. Darwin's father Robert was not a Unitarian, but he was very liberal.

Charles was a pre-divinity student at Cambridge, but Bible studies were not a part of the curriculum at that level. While there, Darwin was influenced by the writing of the liberal Anglican theologian William Paley (1743-1805). During his famous voyage on the *Beagle,* 1831-36, Darwin took a few books along, including Milton's *Paradise Lost,* the Bible, and Lyell's newly published *Principles of Geology,* which accounted for the earth's geological features by natural means over a long time rather than by sudden catastrophic events such as the Flood. As Darwin compiled his notes for publication, what faith he had gave way to doubts.[236]

It is generally held that Darwin hesitated to publish *The Origin of Species* for fear of troubling people in their faith. In *God's Funeral,* A. C. Wilson traces the loss of faith among the Victorians and says of Darwin, "It is doubtful whether he would have gone into print so soon—perhaps at all—had it not been for the fact that another biologist, Alfred Russel Wallace, was on the verge of publishing a paper suggesting a theory of natural selection to explain the evolution of species."[237] It seems at least as likely that his inability to find the key to evolution—natural selection—explains his hesitancy to publish.

---

235 Arnold C. Brackman, *A Delicate Balance: The Strange Case of Charles Darwin and Alfred Russel Wallace* (New York: Times Books, 1980), 199.
236 According to Julian Huxley and H. B. D. Kettlewell, "Within two weeks of leaving England he [Darwin] had commenced to question orthodox beliefs." *Charles Darwin and His World* (New York: Viking, 1965), 23.
237 A. N. Wilson, *God's Funeral* (New York and London: W. W. Norton, 1999), 183-4.

The Origin of Species

The key to *Origins* (1859) is the concept of natural selection. "I am convinced," says Darwin, "that Natural Selection has been the most important, but not the exclusive, means of modification" (30). He goes on to explain that the "preservation of favourable individual differences and variations, and the destruction of those that are injurious, I have called Natural Selection or the Survival of the Fittest" (88). In effect, natural selection afforded a way to explain nature without the supernatural.

Nature, acting blindly, then, takes the place of God. For evidence, Darwin points to the geological record, while admitting that the record, "viewed as a whole, is extremely imperfect" (298). He appeals to morphology and homology, which he defines as "that relation between parts which results from their development from corresponding embryonic parts" (403ff, 456); similar structures suggest similar origins. Such an idea cannot be proved one way or the other.

Darwin also argues that if human beings can selectively breed plants and animals, how much more can Nature. From such micro-changes, he argues for macro-evolution (109). In depicting natural selection, Darwin uses the simile of a tree (129). With the green leaves representing existing species, we can see the development from a common root. While this imagery is helpful in picturing the theory, it does not explain it.

In concluding *The Origin of Species,* Darwin appeals to the Creator, who has "impressed" laws on matter (449). What Darwin has done is develop a closely argued explanation of the biological world on a deistic framework. To shift into another metaphor, God, the great watchmaker, has started the process and now it runs on its own.

The Descent of Man

The Descent of Man (1871) seems less tightly reasoned than *Origin,* as Darwin loosely employs a variety of approaches to his subject.

Analogies play a key role. Detecting similarities between the physical makeup of animals and man, Darwin argues: "The homological construction of the whole frame in the members of the same class is intelligible, if we admit their descent from a common progenitor."[238] *Observations* include Darwin's personal annotations, incorporating inferences from watching his own dog: "He must, I think, have reasoned to himself in a rapid and unconscious manner, that movement without any apparent cause indicated the presence of some strange living agent" (98). *Anthropomorphisms* include, "Many animals, however, certainly sym-

---

[238] Charles Darwin, *The Descent of Man* (Amherst, NY: Prometheus Books, 1998), 96-7. Subsequent references to this work are indicated with page numbers in parentheses in the text.

pathize with each other's distress or danger" (105). *Assertions*—Darwin simply asserts his points, for example: "The fact that the lower animals are excited by the same emotions as ourselves is so well established, that it will not be necessary to weary the reader by many details" (70). While the cumulative effect of these features may appear to be powerful, the individual arguments are not always effective.

Darwin argues there is no natural knowledge of God: "There is no evidence that man was aboriginally endowed with the ennobling belief in the existence of an omnipotent God. . . . " (96-7). He sees civilization as the development toward complexity, as contrasted with the simplicity of what is referred to as savage, barbarian, or lower. He concludes that "man is descended from some lowly organized form . . . there can hardly be a doubt that we are descended from barbarians" (642). Here we find no peon to the Creator, but only the lament that "Man still bears in his bodily frame the indelible stamp of his lowly origin" (643).

Along with Darwin's expression of man's savage origins, came an apparent distaste for Christianity. In an 1873 letter, he wrote:

> Lyell is most firmly convinced that he has shaken the faith in the Deluge far more effectively by never having said a word against the Bible than if he had acted otherwise . . . I have read lately Morley's *Life of Voltaire* and he insists strongly that direct attacks on Christianity . . . produce little permanent effect; real good seems only to follow the slow and silent side attacks.[239]

Darwin did not simply gather information and then come to conclusions on the basis of research. He had been drawn to Malthus's ideas of population growth and from that developed his concept of the struggle for existence. Indeed, he had his ideas before he marshaled his facts.

Autobiography

Darwin's autobiography shows that he held preconceived ideas about what God should be like, ideas that influenced his scientific thinking:

> . . . A being so powerful and so full of knowledge as a God who could create the universe, is to our finite minds omnipotent and omniscient, and it revolts our understanding to suppose that his benevolence is not unbounded, for what advantage can there be in the sufferings of millions of the lower animals throughout almost endless time? This very old argument from the existence of suffering against the existence of an intelligent first cause seems to me a strong one; . . . [240]

This is not a scientific argument, but philosophical and theological. It has been discussed countless times by theologians and philosophers through

---

239 Quoted in Gertrude Himmelfarb, *Darwin and the Darwinian Revolution* (Gloucester, MA: Peter Smith, 1967), 387.
240 Charles Darwin and Thomas Henry Huxley. *Autobiographies,* ed. Gavin de Beer (London: Oxford University Press, 1974), 52.

the ages.[241] Darwin proceeds to relate how in the years since the publication of *Origin*, his faith that there is a God became weaker until he "must be content to remain an Agnostic."[242] He was not alone in this, as W. H. Mallock lamented in 1878, "One may almost say with us one can hear faith decaying."[243]

When Darwin's work was first published, it met with opposition.[244] Yet his theory also met with surprising acceptance among many theologians. It was not until the twentieth century that the Creation-Evolution debate developed in full force.[245]

VICTORIAN VOICES

While Darwin was removing God from creation and the natural world, Karl Marx (1818-83) was doing the same in economics and politics, and Sigmund Freud (1856-1939) would later do in psychology. Along with the poet Tennyson, other Victorian literary voices exemplify just how much that age was the critical transition into the world of today. Two in particular stand out.

Robert Browning's Dramatic Monologues

With the publication of *The Ring and the Book* in 1868-69, Robert Browning (1812-89) joined Tennyson as England's other most highly regarded poet. Much of the enduring power of Browning's poetry comes from his development of characters whose personalities, beliefs, and histories come alive on the printed page in dramatic dialogues. His work abounds with religious themes and allusions, dealing with life and death in relation to eternity. Character after character in Browning's poetry grapples with the issue of how best to use the time one is allotted on earth.

Browning's poems are frequented with little known personages from history or even fictitious characters. His use of second-level characters can be read as the Victorians' struggle with the literary greatness of Milton, Wordsworth, and the other Romantics. Not only were the Victorians unable to come to terms with the illustrious masters of the past, they were also unable to come to terms with their own times. They especially struggled with the loss of religious faith.

---

241 See, for example, Louis P. Pojman, and Lewis Vaughn, *Philosophy The Quest for Truth*, eighth edition (New York and Oxford: Oxford University Press, 2012), 114-130.
242 Darwin and Huxley. *Autobiographies*, 54.
243 Quoted in Wilson, *God's Funeral*, 164.
244 See James R. Moore, *The Post-Darwinian Controversies: A study of the Protestant struggle to come to terms with Darwin in Great Britain and America* (Cambridge: Cambridge University Press, 1979).
245 For the current Intelligent Design debate against Darwinian evolution, see, for example, Michael J. Behe, *Darwin's Black Box: The Biochemical Challenge to Evolution* (New York: The Free Press, 1996); the movie *Expelled: No Intelligence Allowed*, directed by Nathan Frankowski, written by Kevin Miller and Ben Stein (British Columbia: Premise Media, 2008).

Bishop Blougram's Apology

When first published, *Bishop Blougram's Apology* was criticized because of the bishop's "worldliness."[246] Yet the worldly bishop probably was typical of many churchmen in Browning's day, as in our own. His antagonist, Gigadibs, exemplifies the free thinker, whether of Victorian or postmodern times.

Browning depicts the journalist Gigadibs as a one-dimensional figure. This free thinker has rejected both institutional and revealed religion. Roma King captures the character of Gigadibs (and his many clones over the years): "Incapable of intellectual discipline, Gigadibs has acquired a sleek modernity and parrots second-hand ideas like a new convert."[247] Bishop Sylvester Blougram, on the other hand, is a complex character. He is worldly but also spiritual enough to know the superficiality of Gigadibs's simple materialism. Yet the bishop has doubts of his own.

The poem opens with the bishop as the congenial host. As he moves into his apology, he pits faith against unbelief and argues the benefits of the former:

> All we have gained then by our unbelief
> Is a life of doubt diversified by faith,
> For one of faith diversified by doubt;
> We called the chess-board white,—
> we call it black, (lines 209-12)[248]

Faith versus unbelief was *the* great spiritual issue for Victorians. Rather than opting for a leap into sheer emotionalism, the bishop—a la Pascal—makes a sort of wager: " . . . concede to me but the merest chance / Doubt may be wrong—there's judgment, life to come!" (476-7) Even unbelief is a kind of faith, namely, that the believers are wrong. And it, too, has its moments of doubt, that is, of faith. For Blougram, it comes down to the will: "If you desire faith—then you've faith enough" (634-5). Besides, argues the bishop, faith produces an enthusiasm for life that doubt can never create. To prove this, he contrasts Martin Luther with D. F. Strauss, whose *Leben Jesu* questioned the historicity of Jesus:

> Enthusiasm's the best thing, I repeat;
> . . . .
> Why to be Luther—that's a life to lead,
> Incomparably better than my own.

---

246 Roma A. King, Jr., *The Bow and the Lyre: The Art of Robert Browning* (Ann Arbor: University of Michigan Press, 1964), 76.
247 King, *The Bow and the Lyre*, 81.
248 Robert Browning, *Robert Browning's Poetry*, ed. James F. Loucks (New York and London: W. W. Norton, 1979). Subsequent line references are to this edition.

> . . . All Strauss should be
> I might be also. But to what result?
> He looks upon no future; Luther did.
> What can I gain on the denying side?
> Ice makes no conflagration . . .
> Then add there's still that plaguy hundredth chance
> Strauss may be wrong. And so a risk is run—
> For what gain? not for Luther's who secured
> A real heaven in his heart throughout his life,
> Supposing death a little altered thing. (556-91)

Although the bishop only gives a hundredth chance that Strauss may be wrong, he does grant the possibility. He concludes: "The sum of all is—yes, my doubt is great, / My faith's still greater, then my faith's enough" (724-5). Having said that, he says that in serving the church he has lived a life of "comfort" (800). Church work has been good to him in the here and now.

Bishop Blougram mocks the petty literary accomplishments of Gigadibs. The bishop is arrogant and self-serving and lacks the one thing most needful—love. In the words of the apostle Paul, "Knowledge puffs up, but love builds up" (1 Corinthians 8:1).

Although Browning frequently points out the foibles and hypocrisy of ecclesiastical people, he stops short of criticizing the founder of the Christian religion. Minnie Gresham Machen points out, "The evidence of Browning's acceptance of Christ as the Divine Saviour receives confirmation from the fact that disbelief in Christianity is not in a single case expressed by his best characters." [249] That "acceptance of Christ" as Savior is largely an argument from silence.

In the England of Browning's day there were three main religious positions.[250] The first was conservative Protestantism, with its emphasis on individual salvation. The second was epitomized in the Oxford Movement, which "reasserted the role of the church." The third was "rationalistic liberalism," with its roots in the theology of Friederich Schleiermacher, widely recognized as the father of modern liberal theology, with its accommodations to the cultural and scientific thought of the day. Here it seems, Browning, like Bishop Blougram, was most at home.

---

[249] Minnie Gresham Machen, *The Bible in Browning: With Particular Reference to The Ring and the Book* (New York: MacMillan, 1903), 78.

[250] E. LeRoy Lawson, *Very Sure of God: Religious Language in the Poetry of Browning* Nashville: Vanderbilt University Press, 1974), 15-7.

Modern before His Time: Matthew Arnold

The third great Victorian poet, Matthew Arnold (1822-88), is more difficult to classify than Tennyson or Browning. In some ways, Arnold is the *most* enduring writer of the three, enduring because he was ahead of his time in two paradoxical ways. On the one hand, he was ahead of his time in his poetic skepticism. On the other hand, he was modern in his religious liberalism.

Arnold the Poet

Arnold the poet was a skeptic, apparently more ready to let go of faith than either Tennyson or Browning, both of whom struggled to reconcile faith with the times in which they lived.

> Arnold was the famous son of a famous father. Thomas Arnold was the headmaster of Rugby, a leader of the Broad Church school of Liberal Protestantism . . . and a very earnest Victorian who summoned his boys to a life of moral warfare and strenuous work. The son was something of a black sheep. Partly in reaction against this father, he cultivated the elegant airs of a dandy. . . .
>
> The fact is that Arnold's dandyism was largely a mask, . . . For he was suffering from the disease of the nineteenth century, the collapse of traditional beliefs, especially in religion, as the waves of modern thought—science and Utilitarianism and Biblical criticism—broke over his head at Oxford, to leave him . . . in a painful darkness of indecision and doubt.[251]

In *Easter Day, Naples 1849,* Arnold's close friend Arthur Clough included this chant:

> Christ is not risen, no,
>
> He lies and moulders low;
>
> Christ is not risen.
>
> Ashes to ashes, dust to dust;
>
> As of the unjust, also of the just—
>
> Christ is not risen.[252]

Although a subsequent poem by Clough, *Easter Day II,* "affirms the opposite view,"[253] Arnold himself was never to abandon this belief or, rather, unbelief, concerning the central tenet of Christianity.[254] While at Oxford, Arnold heard the great John Henry Newman, who considered liberalism "the halfway house to atheism."[255] Arnold, however, had been introduced to French Romanticism, which reinforced the regard he already had for English Romanticism.

---

251 Spencer, Houghton and Barrows, *British Literature: From Blake to the Present Day,* 715f.
252 As quoted in Wynne-Davis, *Prentice Hall Guide to English Literature,* 255.
253 Wynne-Davis, *Prentice Hall Guide to English Literature,* 255.
254 See Kenneth Allott, ed., *Matthew Arnold.* (Athens, OH: Ohio University Press, 1976), 247.
255 Spencer, Houghton and Barrows, *British Literature: From Blake to the Present Day,* 490.

From the start, Arnold's poetry reflected his desire to build an alternative to Christian faith. We see this, for example, in *Quiet Work*, the introductory poem to his earliest poetry (1849):

> One lesson, Nature, let me learn of thee,
>
> One lesson which in every wind is blown,
>
> One lesson of two duties kept at one
>
> Though the loud world proclaim their enmity.[256]

The poet proceeds to assert that Nature, which outlasts us, teaches us about work.

The Romantic attempt to create a religion without the supernatural was doomed to failure, for nature cannot bear the weight of having to carry the supernatural. It was, as one critic notes, "an attempt to pour the Atlantic into a thimble."[257] Yet in Arnold's second book of poetry (1852), he once again turned to nature. *Lines: Written in Kensington Gardens* is a beautiful little poem. The final two stanzas capture the impact of the poet's apartness from nature:

> Calm soul of all things! Make it mine
>
> To feel, amid the city's jar,
>
> That there abides a peace of thine,
>
> Man did not make, and cannot mar.
>
> The will to neither strive nor cry,
>
> The power to feel with others give!
>
> Calm, calm me more! nor let me die
>
> Before I have begun to live.

In Kensington Gardens, Romanticism sang one of its last winsome songs.

Arnold's *New Poems* in 1867 was his last publication of poetry and contained what was to become his best known poem. No other poem so succinctly expresses the Victorian sense that something had been lost or died, as does *Dover Beach*. It shows the Victorian nostalgia for some bygone era, yet it displays no conviction that the old days were good days. Gone is the Romantic calling to nature for answers. Gone, too, is the heroic figure.

> The sea is calm to-night.
>
> The tide is full, the moon lies fair
>
> Upon the straits;—on the French coast the light
>
> Gleams and is gone; the cliffs of England stand,

---

[256] Matthew Arnold, *Poetry and Criticism of Matthew Arnold*, ed. A. Dwight Culler (Boston: Houghton Mifflin, 1961), 3. Subsequent quotes from Arnold's poetry are from this edition.

[257] David G. James, *Matthew Arnold and the Decline of English Romanticism* (Oxford: Clarendon Press, 1961), 21.

> Glimmering and vast, out on the tranquil bay.
> Come to the window, sweet is the night-air!
> Only, from the lone line of spray
> Where the sea meets the moon-blanch'd land,
> Listen! you hear the grating roar
> Of pebbles which the waves draw back, and fling,
> . . . .
> The Sea of Faith
> Was once, too, at the full, and round earth's shore
> Lay like the folds of a bright girdle furl'd.
> But now I only hear
> Its melancholy, long, withdrawing roar,
> Retreating, to the breath
> Of the night-wind, down the vast edges drear
> And naked shingles of the world.
>
> Ah, love, let us be true
> To one another! for the world, which seems
> To lie before us like a land of dreams,
> So various, so beautiful, so new,
> Hath really neither joy, nor love, nor light,
> Nor certitude, nor peace, nor help for pain;
> And we are here as on a darkling plain
> Swept with confused alarms of struggle and flight,
> Where ignorant armies clash by night.

Except for "the eternal note of sadness," nature is silent; and the heroes have been replaced by ignorant armies clashing in the dark. He anticipated the world of more than a century later, in which whatever value is to be found in life lies in the bond of human relationships: "Ah, love, let us be true . . ." *Dover Beach* is a brilliant statement of the nineteenth century condition. It is an irony of history that Arnold saw faith in retreat at the very time when Christianity—and Protestantism in particular—was in the midst of its "great century" of expansion.[258]

Arnold the Educator

In mid-career Arnold redirected his considerable talents from poetry to education—having become inspector of schools already in 1851 and

---

258 See, for example, Ruth A. Tucker, *From Jerusalem to Irian Jaya: A Biographical History of Christian Missions* (Grand Rapids: Zondervan, 1983), 109-12.

professor of poetry at Oxford in 1858—and to the writing of critical essays. As he grew in his role as England's most noted educator, Arnold saw culture's need for a strong ethical foundation. And that foundation lay in religion.

To Arnold and contemporary intellectuals, the physical resurrection of Jesus from the dead, like other Biblical miracles, was legend, not fact. This meant a radical rethinking of the central tenant of the Christian faith. In his sublime chapter on the resurrection (1 Corinthians 15), the apostle Paul had declared, "And if Christ has not been raised, our preaching is useless and so is your faith. . . . If only for this life we have hope in Christ, we are to be pitied more than all men" (14-19). The challenge facing Arnold was to retain a Christianity without its center. In this, he could fall back on the religion of his father. As it was for his father, the common ground of morality that people have agreed on throughout the years is the basis of religion.

Arnold's wife remarked, "Matt is a good Christian at bottom."[259] More precisely, he was a Christian Humanist, with the emphasis on the latter term. Many who bear the name Christian today hold to Arnold's type of faith, in which doctrine has become marginal and the miraculous largely ruled out. Instead, the emphasis is on moral concerns that cut across denominational lines and span all major religions. Matthew Arnold was truly modern before his time.

AMERICAN EXCURSION: SEA OF LIFE AND SPIRIT

In 1893, at the Parliament of World Religion in Chicago, the dashing Swami Vivekananda arrived from India. He seized the attention of newspapers, and this led to a nationwide speaking tour and the foundation of the Vedanta Society. Also speaking at the convention were Soyen Shaku, a Zen master from Japan, and his interpreter Daisetz T. Suzuki. The Chicago Parliament is often cited as the introduction of Eastern spirituality into America.[260] The century since then has witnessed a growing fascination with Hinduism and Buddhism along with the rise of the New Age Movement. But Eastern monistic thought had already found a home in New England Transcendentalism, in the works of Emerson, Thoreau, and others.

Breathing the atmosphere of nineteenth century New England spirituality, Mary Baker Eddy of Boston produced her famous book *Science and Health*. In 1881, she established the Massachusetts

---
259 As quoted in Allott, *Matthew Arnold*, 236.
260 Arthur. Versluis, *American Transcendentalism & Asian Religions* (New York and Oxford: Oxford University Press, 1993), 216.

Metaphysical College, which became the Christian Science Church, with its downplaying of the material world, denial of sin, and ideas of healing. It was also in this New England atmosphere that Sarah Orne Jewett (1849-1909) grew up, lived, and worked.

Country of the Pointed Firs

Sarah Orne Jewett's *The Country of the Pointed Firs* is a treasure of American literature. [261] Reserved and sparse, like the Maine landscape and its people, the work is moving and dignified. In its emphasis on the interaction between geographical setting and the people who inhabit the region, it is a pure example of regionalism. While depicting the customs and mannerisms of her native Maine, Jewett's writing also operates on a deeper level. It is an expression of her personal spirituality, which was an outgrowth of a worldview that had become a part of the nineteenth century New England spiritual landscape.

Amidst the decaying atmosphere of mainstream nineteenth-century New England Calvinism, new spiritual winds were blowing—winds that at the time were unique to the region. By the early nineteenth century, the passion of the revivals of Jonathan Edwards (1703-58), the "American Calvin," had given way to something akin to the Latitudinarianism that across the Atlantic had created a mellower Anglicanism.

According to Josephine Donovan, Sarah Orne Jewett "was a believing Christian."[262] She grew up in the Congregational Church. Jewett was much impressed with the preaching of Henry Ward Beecher, brother of Harriet Beecher Stowe. Like so many other New Englanders, Jewett's Christianity was anything but doctrinaire. And "like many women writers," she developed a distaste for the strong judgmental theology of the old Calvinism, "that lingered in the New England mind-set long after the sect itself had declined."[263]

That distaste is evident in her portrayal of the Reverend Dimmick in *The Country of the Pointed Firs*. Beginning with his name, Dimmick is portrayed in a most unflattering way. The herbalist Mrs. Todd describes him as "well meanin', but very numb in his feelin's" (65). He is unable to offer comfort to poor Joanna who lives alone on Shell-heap Island. While Joanna has an "old Bible a-layin' on the shelf," Dimmick fails to open it and read it (69). After he has turned his "stupid back," and left Joanna's house, Joanna confides to Mrs. Todd, "I have committed the unpardonable sin" (70). It is significant that this doctrine, the one Biblical doctrine to come to the fore in *The Country of the Pointed Firs*, is shown to have brought sorrow into Joanna's life.

---

261 Sarah Orne Jewett, *The Country of the Pointed Firs and Other Stories* (New York: Anchor Books, 1989). Subsequent quotes from this work are indicated in parentheses in the text.
262 Josephine Donovan, "Jewett and Swedenborg," *American Literature*, 65:4 (December 1993): 731.
263 Donovan, "Jewett and Swedenborg," 731-2.

In a number of places in *The County of the Pointed Firs,* people talk in general terms about singing hymns or going to church, but no particulars are given. In this way, Jewett depicts the old religion of New England. Its representatives and institutions are ineffective or merely serve as a backdrop for more meaningful activities.

Many New England intellectuals moved beyond a dislike for traditional Calvinism and turned to Unitarianism. Among some, such as Emerson, Unitarianism was also being displaced by Transcendentalism, with its monistic view of existence and belief in the indwelling of God in everything. The influence of Transcendentalism is also evident in the work of Jewett's better-known New England contemporary Emily Dickinson (1830-1886), albeit to a lesser degree.[264]

The relation between human beings and nature permeates *The Country of the Pointed Firs*. An example is the story's central character, Mrs. Todd, who busies herself with "rustic simplicities and the scents of primeval herbs" (49). Some twenty-seven herbs indigenous to the region are mentioned, as they heal and help bring lovers together. The herbs also bring Mrs. Todd close to the earth and the mysteries it holds. "There were some strange and pungent odors that roused a dim sense and remembrance of something in the forgotten past. Some of these might have once belonged to sacred and mystic rites, and have had some occult knowledge handed with them down through the centuries" (14). In keeping with the seasons, she lives in cyclical, as opposed to linear, time.[265]

While New England Transcendentalists looked to nature, they also drew from such disparate sources as Plato, Plotinus, Confucius, Islamic Sufis, the Uphanishads, and Buddhism, along with the Bible, Thomas a Kempis, Pascal, and Emanuel Swedenborg. New England writers such as Harriet Beecher Stowe, author of *Uncle Tom's Cabin* and *The Pearl of Orr's Island* (which Jewett singled out as "the most influential work she read as a youth"[266]), and Jewett felt free to incorporate Biblical and other worldviews into their work.

Among Transcendentalism's many sources, Swedenborgianism or the New Church is of particular interest. In a letter to her friend Annie Fields, Jewett wrote, "I wonder how far you have got in the Swedenborg book? I keep a sense of it under everything else. How such a bit of foundation lifts up all one's other thoughts together."[267] Swedenborg seemed to hover everywhere, especially in New England.

---

264   See Jennifer Gage Edison, "Religious Influences on Emily Dickinson: Puritanism and Transcendentalism in Her Poetry," http://itech.fgcu.edu/faculty/wohlpart/alra/edidwell.htm
265   See Margaret Baker Graham, "Visions of Time in *The Country of the Pointed Firs*." *Studies in Short Fiction.* 32:1 (Winter 1995): 29-37.
266   Josephine Donovan, *Sarah Orne Jewett,* (New York: Frederick Ungar, 1980), 8.
267   Sarah Orne Jewett, *Letters of Sarah Orne Jewett,* ed. Annie Fields (Boston and New York: Houghton Mifflin, 1911), 21-2.

The ideas of Swedenborg and Transcendentalism permeate *The Country of the Pointed Firs*. On the novel's opening page, the narrator recounts her return to Dunnet. She compares getting to know the village with "becoming acquainted with a single person," a relationship in which "love at first sight" gives way to a lifelong "growth of true friendship" (13). Though feelings of remoteness come upon the narrator, she sees the place as the center of civilization (13). This dovetails with Transcendentalism's view of the centrality of the individual and the relation between the living world and the inanimate. Civilization—indeed, the universe—is centered in this quiet village. It is all centered in the individual visiting the region.

At a time when many were seeking to break through to the supernatural by attempting to communicate with the dead, Emerson noted, "Whatever spirit is called up—Franklin, or Fenelon, or Napoleon, or Abd-el-Kader—it is always Swedenborg that answers."[268] The nineteenth century belief in spirits and contact with them was widespread; it was a belief that Jewett shared. It appears in *The Country of the Pointed Firs,* when Jewett has Captain Littlepage describe a voyage in which a crew saw strange apparitions, hovering between this world and another.

Jewett injects into the novel a sense of the mysterious, an almost timeless world hovering between past and present, and between the mind and the object, between matter and spirit. "While the fascination with the supernatural is characteristically New England, . . . Jewett's interest seems finally to go beyond the level of the ghost story."[269] She focuses on the concept of monism—all is one. For Jewett, the whole of nature is divine. As the narrator and Mrs. Todd stand looking at the harbor and the islands, the narrator notes, "The sunburst upon that outermost island made it seem like a sudden revelation of the world beyond this which some believe to be so near" (33). It is not ghostly figures that link this world with another. It is nature itself.

The ocean surrounding the islands is more than a mere symbol of infinity. It is infinite. From the highest point on Green Island, the narrator and William look beneath them. "[We] could see the ocean that circled this and a hundred other bits of island-ground, the mainland shore and all the far horizons. It gave a sudden sense of space, for nothing stopped the eye or hedged one in,—that sense of liberty in space and time which great prospects always give" (46). Following this, they join William's sister and mother for dinner. The first thing William does on entering the house is "wash his hands like a pious Brahmin." Here, the Eastern worldview dominates. In Transcendental monism the soul of each individual

---
268 As quoted in Slater Brown, *The Heyday of Spiritualism* (New York: Hawthorn Books, 1970), 214.
269 Josephine Donovan, "A Woman's Vision of Transcendence: A New Interpretation of the Works of Sarah Orne Jewett," *The Massachusetts Review* 21 (Summer 1980): 380.

"is identical with the soul of the world."[270] Each person has the potential of embodying a universe.

Joanna was in harmony with nature, while the minister was out of tune with it. In one critic's words, Dimmick represents "Calvinism or other civilizational theology."[271] Joanna and the birds were at one with nature, and in its singing on her coffin the bird seems to express a hope for immortality. Nature corresponds to the world of human beings—and vice-versa. On the islands, "the trees seemed to march seaward" (33). Elsewhere, the sea and sky are described as being given to "calms and passions" (75). From a literary standpoint, these are examples of personification, a figure of speech; but in *The Country of the Pointed Firs* they go beyond that.

The concept of the interconnectedness of all things is reflected in the powerful scene in which the narrator leaves Dunnet Landing. "I stood on deck, looking back, and watched the busy gulls agree and turn . . . The sea was full of life and spirit, the tops of the waves flew back as if they were winged like the gulls themselves, and like them had the freedom of the wind" (161).

Passing of the Old Order

The intertwining of region and religion is essential to Jewett's work. Transcendentalism was a New England phenomenon, having risen out of the intellectual and spiritual climate of that region. Conservative Christianity was moving west; the Midwest, for example, would become the center of the old, confessional Lutheranism brought by German and Scandinavian immigrants. Catholicism held sway in New Orleans. And fundamentalism was arising through much of the South. Jewett wrote from the standpoint of a religious-intellectual-literary movement that had captured the imagination of many in New England.

Jewett enlisted a worldview that was relatively fresh to New England—and largely untreated throughout the rest of the country—to elegize the passing of an old way of life. Steamers were replacing schooners, and quaint old village ways were giving way to modern industrial life. At book's end, the narrator wistfully looks back at Dunnet Landing, at a New England that is passing away. Her final words are, "Dunnet Landing and all its coasts were lost to sight" (160).

---

270   James D. Hart, *The Oxford Companion to American Literature,* Sixth edition (New York and Oxford: Oxford University Press, 1995), 674.
271   Graham, "Visions of Time in *The Country of the Pointed Firs,*" 36.

TRUTH AND ART AT THE END OF THE NINETEENTH CENTURY

> Oh roses for the flush of youth,
> And laurel for the perfect prime;
> But pluck an ivy branch for me
> Grown old before my time.[272]

As religion receded under attacks of higher criticism and science, many turned elsewhere to find meaning, truth, and beauty. Christina Georgina Rossetti (1830-94), quoted above, was intensely pious. Moreover, her work radiated with personal emotions, a trait that marked the Pre-Raphaelite movement, in which she and her brother Dante Gabriel Rossetti played key roles. Such emphasis on subjective feelings was a characteristic that set the Pre-Raphaelites at odds with the highly technical but spiritually and emotionally empty productions of much of the Victorian age. Among those influenced by the Pre-Raphaelite group was Walter Horatio Pater (1839-94), who shared their devotion to beauty.

Walter Pater and Aesthetics

Along with Matthew Arnold, the other major critic of the Victorian period, Pater, has had tremendous influence on aesthetics. Pater, who was a wonderful stylist, considered criticism itself a work of art, and he saw art itself as life. He was keenly focused on life's brevity and flux, as he quoted from Plato: "Somewhere Heraclitus says that everything changes and nothing remains."[273] In *Studies in the History of the Renaissance,* Pater writes:

> It is with the movement, the passage and dissolution of impressions, images, sensations, that analysis leaves off—that continual vanishing away, that strange perpetual weaving and unweaving of ourselves.... Not the fruit of experience, but experience itself is the end.... How can we pass most swiftly from point to point, and be present always at the focus where the greatest number of vital forces unite in their purest energy? To burn always with this hard gemlike flame, to maintain this ecstasy, is success in life.... [W]e have an interval, and then our place knows us no more. Some spend this interval in listlessness, some in high passions, the wisest in art and song. For our one chance is in expanding that interval, in getting as many pulsations as possible into the given time.[274]

Influenced by the French "art for art's sake" movement and by the English Pre-Raphaelites, with their emphasis on feeling, Pater saw art as

---
272 Christina Georgina Rossetti, "Song," *The Pre-Raphaelites and Their Circle,* Cecil Y. Lang, ed. (Chicago and London: University of Chicago Press, 1975), 156.
273 From Plato's *Cratylus,* as quoted by Walter Pater, *Studies in the History of the Renaissance,* in Adams, *Critical Theory since Plato,* 642.
274 Pater, *Studies in the History of the Renaissance,* 642-3.

the source of that "hard gemlike flame" that serves as an antidote to the fragmentation of the individual and brings intensity to life.[275]

Sixteen years after his *History of the Renaissance*, Pater would write, "[If good art] be devoted further to the increase of men's happiness, to the redemption of the oppressed, or the enlargement of our sympathies with each other . . . or immediately, as with Dante, to the glory of God, it will also be great art."[276] Pater had come full cycle. At its best, art is not detached from ethical, spiritual issues, but is tied to them. One gets the impression, however, that these religious longings of his later years had more to do with the church's aesthetics than with her doctrines. Yet he did look toward beauty and goodness that exist beyond the flux.

Oscar Wilde

The most noted of Walter Pater's disciples was the dramatist, poet, novelist, and essayist Oscar Wilde (1856-1900). Already as a student at Oxford, Wilde became known as an outstanding classical scholar. He also became notorious as he applied the ideals of aestheticism to his entire lifestyle and evoked the suspicion and distain of society. Wilde is best known for his novel *The Picture of Dorian Grey* (1891), the play *Importance of Being Earnest* (1895), and the account related to his two-year sentence to jail *Ballad of Reading Gaol* (1898).

In *The Decay of Lying* (1889), Wilde sets forth the notion of art-for-art's sake. Art exists in a sphere of its own and needs no practical justification: "The only beautiful things, as somebody [Kant] once said, are the things that do not concern us. As long as a thing is useful or necessary to us . . . it is outside the proper sphere of art."[277] Nor is the beautiful contingent upon facts: "Now everything is changed. Facts are not merely finding a footing place in history, but they are usurping the domain of fancy and have invaded the kingdom of romance" (663).

The artist must put art back in its proper place: "Literature always anticipates life. It does not copy it, but molds it to its purpose" (665). Insofar as art truthfully reflects life, it is a failure; but in running counter to experience—that is, in lying—it serves its proper creative purpose. He ends this essay: "At twilight nature becomes a wonderfully suggestive effect, and is not without loveliness, though perhaps its chief use is to illustrate quotations from the poets" (670).

In *The Critic as Artist* (1891), Wilde further develops his notions of art and truth. In this he goes beyond Pater, to whom he refers as "the

---

275   See "Walter Pater and the Self," in Mary R. Anderson, *Art in a Desacralized World: Nineteenth Century France and England* (New York: University Press of America, 1984), 111-30.
276   As quoted in Iain Fletcher, *Walter Pater* (London: Longmans, Green., 1959), 33-4. The quote originally appeared in Pater's *Appreciations: With an Essay on Style*, published in 1889.
277   Oscar Wilde, "The Decay of Lying," in Adams, *Critical Theory since Plato*, 661. Page numbers of subsequent quotations from this work are noted in the text.

most perfect master of prose now creating among us."[278] For Wilde, art is life—"great works of art are ... in fact, the only things that live" (164).

Wilde uses criticism in a double sense, referring both to the critic and to the artist, for what is art itself but a "criticism of life"? (125) Moreover, it is more difficult to be a critic than an artist, for "criticism demands infinitely more cultivation than creation does" (130). To the artist and critic belong the task of rewriting history and showing humanity the way. This progress means a constant going against the grain of accepted mores of any given age. This sets Wilde at odds, for example, with the ideal of self-denial ("simply a method by which man arrests his progress") and self-sacrifice ("a survival of the mutilation of the savage, part of that old worship of pain") (135).

It is up to literature in particular to create "from the rough material of existence, a new world that will be more marvelous, more enduring, and more true than the world that common eyes look upon" (141). Emotional intensity and joy give life its drive, yet when we look back on such moments they appear as dreams and illusions. Art is what remains. We can constantly return to a work of art to find and feel those all-important emotions. That the aesthetic critic might spend his or her life moving from one mood to another for Wilde is not a problem, but the goal: "We are never more true to ourselves than when we are inconsistent" (191).

Truth, then, is a constant state of becoming. In religious matters, Wilde sees it as "the opinion that has survived," in science "the ultimate sensation," and in art "one's last mood" (194). In this world where beauty is worshipped, "[t]here is no sin except stupidity," and "[t]he artistic critic, like the mystic, is an antinomian always" (221). Wilde declares the nineteenth century "a turning point in history." This he attributes to the work of two men: "Darwin and Renan, the one the critic of the Book of Nature, the other the critic of the books of God" (222). It seemed that the two had put the final pieces together in the great project that the Enlightenment had undertaken—namely to remove the God of history from his role as Creator and Revealer. Darwin did it by explaining creation on the basis of natural selection, while Joseph Ernest Renan (1823-92) had taken the Scriptures off the pedestal as a special divine revelation.

Wilde had special interest in Christ, the "supreme artist" and his relation to sinners. In *De Profundis,* written while Wilde was imprisoned for sodomy in 1897, he expressed his views:

> The world had always loved the saint as being the nearest possible approach to the perfection of God. Christ, through some divine instinct in him, seems to have always loved the sinner as being the nearest possible approach to the perfection of man ... To turn an interesting thief into a tedious honest man was not his aim ... The

---

278 Oscar Wilde, "The Critic as Artist," in Adams, *Critical Theory since Plato,* 117. Page numbers of subsequent quotations from this work are noted in the text.

conversion of a publican into a Pharisee would not have seemed to him a great achievement. But in a manner not yet understood of the world he regarded sin and suffering as being in themselves beautiful holy things and modes of perfection.[279]

Wilde's language does not reflect that of the Scriptures. For Christ honesty was not tedious. He had an interest in converting both interesting thieves and Pharisees into God's children. In his parable of the Pharisee and the publican in the temple, Jesus says the difference between the two was not that one was a sinner and the other was not, since both were sinners. Rather, it was a matter of honesty: "For everyone who exalts himself will be humbled, and he who humbles himself will be exalted" (Luke 18:14). Christ's death on the cross was not a testimony to the beauty of sin, but to its horror. This is what grace is all about, that for some unfathomable reason, God loved sinful human beings not because of their sin but in spite of it.

Friedrich Nietzsche

If Oscar Wilde is the dazzling yet somewhat flighty apologist of the religion of aesthetics, the classicist-philosopher Friedrich Nietzsche (1844-1900) is the thundering voice from the heights. We will look at two short essays—"Truth and Falsity in an Ultramoral Sense" (1873)[280] and "The Acceptance of Untruth" (1882),[281]—and selections from *The Will to Power* (1886).[282]

"When we talk about trees, colors, snow, and flowers, we believe we know something about the things themselves," wrote Nietzsche in "Truth and Falsity in an Ultramoral Sense," and "yet we only possess metaphors of the things, and these metaphors do not in the least correspond to the original essential" (635). He asks, "What therefore is truth?" and answers, "A mobile army of metaphors, metonymies, anthropomorphisms: in short a sum of human relations . . ." (636).

The prevailing set of symbols—that is, the art—by which a society operates and which it takes as its truth are the concepts that belong to the strongest and victorious people. Their "art can establish her rule over life" (639). In "The Acceptance of Untruth" from *The Joyful Wisdom*, Nietzsche further puts forward the relation of art to truth: "If we had not approved of the Arts and invented this sort of cult into the untrue, the insight into the general untruth and falsity of things now given us by science . . . would be quite unendurable" (98).

---

279 As quoted in G. Wilson Knight, "Christ and Wilde," in *Oscar Wilde,* Harold Bloom, ed. (New York: Chelsea House, 1985), 42.
280 Friedrich Nietzsche, "Truth and Falsity in an Ultramoral Sense," in Adams, *Critical Theory since Plato,* 634-9. Page numbers of quotations from this work are noted in the text.
281 Friedrich Nietzsche, "The Acceptance of Untruth," in *The Modern Tradition: Backgrounds of Modern Literature,* Richard Ellmann and Charles Feidelson, ed. (New York: Oxford University Press, 1965), 98-9. Page numbers of quotations from this work are noted in the text
282 Friedrich Nietzsche, *The Will to Power: Prelude to a Philosophy of the Future.* Walter Kaufmann, trans. (New York: Vintage Books, 1966). Page numbers of quotations from this work are noted in the text.

For Nietzsche, skepticism, while unendurable in its stark reality, is the source of human greatness: "Freedom from all kinds of convictions, to be able to see freely, is part of strength" (99). Numerous figures from history that would seem to contradict this come to mind. As for the likes of Germany's own Luther, he was a "northern barbarian of the spirit" (60). No matter what their achievement, any who are attached to religion in general and Christianity in particular have entered a state of "enslavement and self-mockery" (60). Nietzsche looked to the day when the concepts of God and sin—"will seem no more important to us than a child's toy" (69).

Nietzsche did not live to see the day when millions would suffer and die at the hands of secular ideologies. Significantly, his argument with Christianity was not that it is not true, but that he saw it as inhibitive of personal fulfillment: "Christianity gave Eros poison to drink: he did not die of it but degenerated—into a vice" (92). For Nietzsche, truth was not really in the picture. Truth is merely what has become accepted as such. "*Genuine philosophers, however, are commanders and legislators*: they say, '*thus* it *shall* be!'" (emphasis original, 136)

While expressed more vigorously, his notion of truth is like that of Pater and Wilde. It is the creation of the great man, who declares the dawning of a new day of celebration—as symbolized by Zarathustra—when the old dualities of darkness and light, good and evil will be merged.

> Sure of our victory, we celebrate
>> The feast of feasts:
> Friend Zarathustra come, the guest of guests!
> The world now laughs, rent are the drapes of fright,
> The wedding is at hand of dark and light— (245)

Transitions

Many others would espouse the notion of art as truth. Rudyard Kipling (1865-1936) is a case in point. His "Ballad of East and West" begins and ends with the famous lines:

> Oh, East is East, and West is West, and never the twain shall meet,
> Till Earth and Sky stand presently at God's great Judgment Seat;
> But there is neither East nor West, Border, nor Breed, nor Birth,
> When two strong men stand face to face, though they come from the ends of the earth!

Kipling speaks of the friendship between the leader of a tribe in northern India and the son of a British colonel; they take an oath of blood brothers that transcends nationality or creed.[283]

If the likes of Walter Pater experienced a turn-around, others did not. His contemporary Algernon Charles Swinburne (1837-1909) shocked readers with attacks on Christianity. Echoing words attributed to the Roman Emperor Julian the Apostate, Swinburne's *Hymn to Proserpine* laments, "Thou hast conquered, O pale Galilean; the world has grown grey from thy breath."

Whether manifesting itself subtly or in frontal attacks on Christianity, by the late nineteenth century a new world was well under construction. In this realignment, the concept of the role of aesthetics had shifted drastically. Aesthetics, the realm of art, had shifted from being a servant or, at times, an obstacle to the real values, and become an end in itself.

This shift paralleled a changing concept of the world itself. The material world along with its beauty and sublimity had become all encompassing. The Beyond had been emptied of its mystery, its unfathomableness, its otherness and sacredness. The here and now is all we have. As Swinburne says at poem's end: "For there is no God found stronger than death."[284]

---

283   Rudyard Kipling, *Rudyard Kipling's Verse* (Garden City, NY: Doubleday, 1927), 268-72.
284   Lang, *The Pre-Raphaelites*, 358-60.

PART 5
THE AGE OF MODERNISM AND BEYOND: 1900—THE PRESENT

REVOLT OF THE SOUL: WILLIAM BUTLER YEATS

"The mystical life is at the center of all that I think and all that I write.... I have always considered myself a voice of what I believe to be a greater renaissance—the revolt of the soul against the intellect—now beginning in the world."[285]

Nineteenth century Europe into which William Butler Yeats (1865-1939) was born was the scene of huge upheavals. Seeds sown in the winds of the Enlightenment were now reaping the whirlwind:

> In the nineteenth century the Christian faith found itself challenged from three directions: from science in the shape of the theory of evolution, from philosophy in the form of alternative world-views intended to make belief in God obsolete, and from history in the guise of biblical criticism.[286]

Throughout the century the Old Testament scriptures had come under heavy attacks. The most influential Bible critic was the German scholar Julius Wellhausen (1844-1910), who concluded that the Hebrew religion had evolved from primitive nomadic stories. He and others saw the Old Testament as a patchwork compiled by unknown editors. As for the New Testament, the 1860s saw J. E. Renan in France and J. R. Seeley in England follow Strauss's lead and view the supernatural and messianic elements in the four Gospels as myth rather than real history.

Madame Blavatsky

This was the world of John Butler Yeats, the son of an Irish clergyman and the father of the poet. JBY rejected his father's faith and arrived at "the conclusion that revealed religion was myth and fable."[287] In spite of such facts, some writers still characterize the poet's

---
285 As quoted in George Mills Harper, *Yeats's Golden Dawn* (London: Macmillan, 1974), 2.
286 Dowley, *Eerdmans' Handbook to the History of Christianity*, 544.
287 Richard Ellmann, *Yeats: The Man and the Masks* (New York: W. W. Norton, 1979), 10.

background as one that was "solid prosaically Protestant Church of Ireland."[288] William was raised not in the faith of his grandfather, but in the skepticism of his father.

There was, however, another side to the family, a side to which Yeats quickly turned. The young WBY spent much time with and became close with his uncle, George Pollexfen, who was fascinated by magic and astrology. And Yeats's aunt, Isabella Pollexfen, first sent him a copy of A. P. Sinnett's *Esoteric Buddhism,* an endorsement of the teachings of Sinnett's friend Madame Blavatsky. Yeats and a fellow high school student, Charles Johnston, who also read the book, founded the Dublin Hermetic Society.

"All over Europe and America," notes Richard Ellmann, "young men dropped like him, and usually without his caution, into the treacherous currents of semi-mystical thought. They refused to accept the universe that their scientific, materialist, rationalist, and often hypocritically religious elders tried to hand them."[289] People were turning to the occult.

Viewing itself the heir of ancient wisdom, occultism calls upon its initiates to maintain their role as guardians of that wisdom through secrecy. No one made more effective use of occultic "alliances" than Helena Petrovna Blavatsky, known as Madame Blavatsky, whom Yeats began to visit in London in 1887. Blavatsky was the founder of Theosophy, an occult system teaching that a "red thread" runs through all religions and that all life is one.

Blavatsky's influence has increased with time. The founder of what began as a small esoteric movement, she continues as a formative figure of culture. One scholar remarks:

> Certainly she believed that the West had better look to the East, if it wanted to learn what real philosophy was (or to relearn what it once knew). With equal certainty she despised every form of institutional Christianity. As a result, her Society, its members, and its offshoots became the main vehicle for Buddhist and Hindu philosophies to enter the Western consciousness.... Together with the Western occult tradition, the Theosophists have provided almost all the underpinnings of the 'New Age'... to plunge humanity into the spiritual alembic in which we find ourselves today.[290]

None of that would come within the lifetime of Blavatsky, who died in 1891. Nor would Yeats live to see it. Actually, Yeats's direct participation in the Theosophical Society lasted less than three years. About the time Yeats was leaving the society, a twenty-one-year-old Indian law student named Mohandas Gandhi had begun visiting Madame Blavatsky's London lodge and would be leaving with a renewed appreciation of his Hindu roots.

---

288 Graham Hough, *The Mystery Religion of W. B. Yeats* (Sussex: Harvester Press, 1984), 31.
289 Ellmann, *Yeats,* 58.
290 Joscelyn Godwin, *The Theosophical Enlightenment* (Albany: State University of New York Press, 1994), 379.

The Golden Dawn

When he left the Theosophical Society, Yeats had already been initiated into the Order of the Golden Dawn. To enter the system Tarot cards were used. For Yeats, the material world "is but a symbolic image," while "the invisible world is the real."[291]

During his years in the Golden Dawn, Yeats, through seances, came into contact with the invisible world through a spirit named Leo Africanus. This spirit was Yeats's opposite, his alter-ego. The unscrupulous Leo Africanus served as a foil for the cautious Yeats. Everything became antitheses: Yeats and Leo Africanus, Hic and Ille, Discord and Concord. Each member of the order had a motto, and Yeats's was "Demon Est Deus Inversus" ("The demon is God inverted"). Yeats would sign correspondence with D. E. D. I. His life was saturated with the occult:

> A mere listing of the forms it took is impressive: they include native Irish fairy lore and Druidism; Theosophical studies; participation in the Order of the Golden Dawn . . . and attempts to found an Irish order, the Castle of the Heroes; Boehme, Swedenborg, and Blake; magic; astrology and the casting of horoscopes; Indian (i.e. Hindu) lore; seances; and the Tarot cards.[292]

In considering what Yeats's religion or philosophy was, it is also important to see what it was not. It was not the materialistic rationalism of his father. Yet both father and son dismissed Christianity. "Like Blake and Shelley," notes Bloom, "Yeats sets himself against the 'system' of Christendom, . . . And he sets himself also against Christian love."[293] For Yeats the Christian concept of love, like that of salvation and the other doctrines, was dispensable. Rather, "Yeats's love is a cold passion."[294] Nor did he believe in that divine love from God known as grace.[295]

Centuries earlier, Augustine noted that seekers of great acuteness and ability in the school of Plotinus either "were corrupted by curious inquiries into magic" or "passed into the service of Christ."[296] For Yeats, a student of Plotinus, the latter never was an option. Like Shelley before him, Yeats believed that it was for "poets and artists" once more to begin carrying "the burdens that priests and theologians took from them angrily some few hundred years ago."[297]

---

291 Harper, *Yeats's Golden Dawn*, 75.
292 Weldon Thornton, "Between Circle and Straight Line: A Pragmatic View of W. B. Yeats and the Occult," *Studies in the Literary Imagination*, 14 (Spring 1981): 62-3.
293 Harold Bloom, *Yeats*, (Oxford and New York, Oxford University Press, 1970), 283.
294 Bloom, *Yeats*, 284.
295 Harper, *Yeats's Golden Dawn*, 73.
296 Augustine, "Letter CXVIII," 3,17 in *St. Augustine*, vol. 1, ed. Philip Schaff (Grand Rapids: Eerdmans, 1956), 450.
297 William Butler Yeats, *Essays and Introductions* (New York: Macmillan, 1961), 64.

Yeats's Work

The mystical-occult motif is evident in Yeats's work; there is no mention of a personal God or revealed scriptures, themes quite outside the Eastern-occult world view. Five poems that span Yeats's career and represent various stages of his life and work bear this out.[298]

The Stolen Child (1886)

Come away, O human child!
To the waters and the wild
With a faery, hand in hand,
For the world's more full of weeping than you
    can understand.

....

The setting is western Ireland. The faeries of Irish folklore seem like mischievous, even amoral children, but when children actually surrender to their enticements, it means an end to the life they had. This could be a separation from their former activities, or actual death for the children. According to Blavatsky, faeries "are the principal agents of disembodied but *never visible* spirits at seances."[299] In 1888, Yeats wrote to the poet Katherine Tynan, "[M]y poetry . . . is almost all a flight into fairy land, from the real world . . ."[300] In Yeats's later life and work, faeries recede from the picture, only to be replaced by the daemons.

The Folly of Being Comforted (1902)

One that is ever kind said yesterday
'Your well-beloved's hair has threads of grey,
And little shadows come about her eyes;
Time can but make it easier to be wise
Though now it seem impossible, and so
All that you need is patience.'
                      Heart cries , 'No,
I have not a crumb of comfort, not a grain.
....
O heart! O heart! if she'd but turn her head,
You'd know the folly of being comforted.

---

298   The poems and other poetic citations are taken from William Butler Yeats, *Selected Poems and Three Plays*, ed. M. L. Rosenthal (New York: Macmillan, 1986).
299   Helen Petrovna Blavatsky, *Isis Unveiled: A Master Key to the Mysteries of Ancient and Modern Science and Theology*, 2 volumes (Pasadena: Theosophical University Press, 1960), 1: xxixf.
300   Daniel Albright, *W.B. Yeats: The Poems* (London: J. M. Dent and Sons, 1990), 424.

A decade before writing this poem, Yeats had expressed his frustration over being "deeply in love with" Maude Gonne, and had gone on to recount: "I threw the Tarot, and when the Fool came up, which means that nothing at all would happen, I turned my mind away. And yet I longed to rid my mind of an obsession that was eating into my mind and beginning to affect my health."[301] In "The Folly of Being Comforted" we see that obsession still at work. It has been suggested that the poem's threefold structure is reminiscent of Job and his three comforters. The suffering Job did find solace; he repented of the folly of questioning God's wisdom (Job 42), and "the Lord blessed the latter part of Job's life more than the first" (42:12). Not so with Yeats.

The Magi (1914)

Now as at all times I can see in the mind's eye,

In their stiff, painted clothes, the pale unsatisfied ones

Appear and disappear in the blue depth of the sky

With all their ancient faces like rain beaten stones,

And all their helms of silver hovering side by side,

And all their eyes still fixed, hoping to find once more,

Being by Calvary's turbulence unsatisfied,

The uncontrollable mystery on the bestial floor.

For many, the poem's title brings to mind the Magi who visited the Christ Child, and the reference to Calvary alludes to his later crucifixion. Yet the poet immediately adds the word "unsatisfied." As Yeats would later write in his play *The Resurrection,* Jesus "was nothing more than a man" and the disciples merely "dogs who have lost their master."[302]

In the Tarot system, the Magus is the magician. While the Magi appear and disappear—in cyclical, gyre-like manner—they have but one focus: "The uncontrollable mystery on the bestial floor." Yeats elaborates in *A Vision*: "When the old primary becomes the new antithetical, the old realisation of an objective moral law is changed into a subconscious turbulent instinct. The world of rigid custom and law is broken up by 'the uncontrollable mystery upon the bestial floor.'"[303] What the Magi await is a new revelation.

Sailing to Byzantium (1927)

That is no country for old men. The young

In one another's arms, birds in the trees

---

301 William Butler Yeats, *Memoirs* (New York: Macmillan, 1972), 78-9.
302 Albright, *W.B. Yeats: The Poems,* 545.
303 William Butler Yeats, *A Vision* (New York: Macmillan/Collier, 1966), 105.

> Those dying generationsat their song,
> The salmon-falls, the mackerel-crowded seas,
> Fish, flesh, or fowl, commend all summer long
> Whatever is begotten, born, and dies.
> Caught in that sensual music all neglect
> Monuments of unageing intellect.
>
> . . . .
>
> Once out of nature I shall never take
> My bodily form from any natural thing,
> But such a form as Grecian goldsmiths make
> Of hammered gold and gold enamelling
> To keep a drowsy Emperor awake;
> Or set upon a golden bough to sing
> To lords and ladies of Byzantium
> Of what is past, or passing, or to come.

In his book *A Vision,* Yeats said about Byzantium: "I think if I could be given a month of Antiquity and leave to spend it where I chose, I would spend it in Byzantium a little before Justinian opened St. Sophia and closed the Academy of Plato. . . . in early Byzantium, maybe never before or since in recorded history, religious, aesthetic and practical life were one."[304]

Given Yeats's distaste for Christianity, we wonder how much he really would have liked the city with its eighty-five monasteries and theologian-emperor Justinian. Yet, the old poet longs to leave Ireland, and sail to Christian Byzantium. There everything comes together in a Theosophical unity. In Byzantium a bird fashioned by goldsmiths sings to a drowsy Emperor or to lords and ladies. We sense in this beautiful poem an indefinable melancholy, as if after all the years of trying the poet has not moved much beyond the skepticism of his father.

Politics (1939)

In our time the destiny of man presents its meanings in political terms. Thomas Mann

> How can I, that girl standing there,
> My attention fix
> On Roman or on Russian
> Or on Spanish politics?

---

304 Yeats, *A Vision,* 279.

> Yet here's a traveled man that knows
> What he talks about,
> And there's a politician
> That has both read and thought,
> And maybe what they say is true
> Of war and war's alarms,
> But O that I were young again
> And held her in my arms.

This was one of Yeats's last poems, written May 23, 1938, eight months before he died. It brings to mind Yeats's own words in his prologue to *A Vision,* "The Phases of the Moon": "All dreams of the soul / End in a beautiful man's or woman's body."[305] For Yeats spiritual concerns and physical love were never far apart: "my imagination runs from Daimon to sweetheart."[306] And sex is not far from politics. In a monistic view of life, nothing is far removed from the feelings of the moment. Nor is there any feeling much stronger than that of lust. The expression of such basic desires is a form of "reasserting the sacredness of the earth."[307]

Renaissance

W. H. Auden, who had written an elegy of Yeats also wrote, "How on earth, we wonder, could a man of Yeats's gifts take such nonsense seriously?"[308] But he did. What Auden saw as "nonsense" places Yeats in the vanguard of modern thought and at the center of today's world. It is telling, for instance, that Yeats is discussed in Robert James Waller's popular *The Bridges of Madison County* and the subsequent movie starring Clint Eastwood and Meryl Streep.

The frustrated country housewife Francesca Johnson has just met the traveling photographer Robert Kincaid, when we are told:

> He looked upward, hands in his Levi's pockets, camera hanging against his left hip. "The silver apples of the moon/The golden apples of the sun." His midrange baritone said the words like that of a professional actor.
>
> She looked over at him. "W. B. Yeats, 'The Song of Wandering Aengus.'"
>
> "Right. Good stuff. Realism, economy, sensuousness, beauty, magic. Appeals to my Irish heritage."
>
> He had said it all, right there in five words. Francesca had labored to explain Yeats to the Winterset students, but never got through to most of them.[309]

---

305 Albright, *W.B. Yeats: The Poems,* 845.
306 William Butler Yeats, *Mythologies* (New York: Macmillan, 1959), 336.
307 Patrick J. Keane, "Yeats's Counter-Enlightenment," *Salmagundi* 68-69 (Fall-Winter 1985-86): 145.
308 Hough, *The Mystery Religion of W. B. Yeats,* 6.
309 Robert James Waller, *The Bridges of Madison County* (New York: Warner Books, 1992), 59-60.

The two have an affair, having disregarded the conventional morality of her small farming community. The story's underlying ideas are Yeatsian, as when Kincaid speaks of "God or the universe or whatever one chooses to label the great systems of balance and order."[310]

In his sonnet "Leda and the Swan," Yeats recounts the Greek myth of Leda being seduced and raped by Zeus in the form of a swan. The union resulted in the birth of Helen—better known as Helen of Troy. This marked the birth of ancient Greek civilization, even as the coming of the Holy Spirit—represented by the dove—upon the Virgin Mary marked the birth of Jesus and the Christian Church. Yeats anticipated the "antithetical flux" of *A Vision*—a return to paganism. Although unnoticed by most, the turning has been real. And swift. Already in the 1970s, one Christian writer noted, "In Great Britain it is estimated that 50 percent of the people are involved in some way with the occult. In contrast to this, about 2 percent attend church."[311]

It is an interesting footnote of history that the Latin term *paganus* originally stood for what was of the countryside or village. By the fourth century, it came to be applied to the people or things related to the old polytheism. There in the villages, Yeats tells us, people still build small cabins. And there grow enchanted trees with berries that are both empowering and poisonous. There the water laps on the shore, and, as the Dove flies away, the Swan returns.

GERMAN EXCURSION: FROM BABEL TO BERLIN

The city of Babel is mentioned early in the Bible. Its name, meaning "Gate of God," first occurs in Genesis 10:10. The city was located in the land of Shinar (ancient Babylonia, modern Iraq), on the banks of the Euphrates River. Babel has become known throughout history as the site of the famous tower. According to the Biblical account, the city's inhabitants declared, "Come, let us build ourselves a city, with a tower that reaches to the heavens, so that we may make a name for ourselves" (Genesis 11:4). The tower was never completed. The Lord "scattered them from there over all the earth" and "confused the language of the whole world" (Genesis 11:8, 9). The term Babel is also a play on a Hebrew word meaning "confusion" or "mixture," a reminder of divine punishment for the pride displayed in its building.

The city of Babylon (which also means "Gate of God") arose on the site. Under King Nebuchadnezzar (605-562 B.C.), the city attained its greatest splendor as capital of the Babylonian Empire. Central to

---

310 Waller, *The Bridges of Madison County*, 141.
311 David W. Hoover, *How to Respond to the Occult* (St. Louis: Concordia, 1977), 8.

Babylon's life was its gods; chief among them were Marduk, ruler of the winds and storms, and Ishtar, goddess of love and war. Under Nebuchadnezzar, the Babylonian army destroyed Jerusalem along with its temple and took the Jews into captivity. Babylon became a Biblical symbol for enemies of God and his people.

The city of Berlin, located on Germany's Spree River, is far removed from Babylon in time and space. First mentioned in 1244, it lay on the northeast edge of the Holy Roman Empire. Over the centuries, Berlin grew in importance. During the German Reformation, Protestant teachings took hold. In 1539 the Reformation came to the city of Berlin. Since then, "the spiritual climate and the atmosphere of this city . . . [had] four hundred years of uninterrupted Protestantism."[312] Not until 1747 was another Catholic church built in Berlin, St. Hedwig's Cathedral.

More religious change transpired in the centuries following the Reformation. Biblical faith gave way to reliance on the natural sciences. "Practical social and political movements came to the fore . . . and a materialistic philosophy seemed to satisfy every need."[313] As an illustration of this, in 1911 Adolf von Harnack (1851-1930) founded the Kaiser-Wilhelm-Gesellschaft, a scientific research institute in a suburb of Berlin.[314] Even so, following the devastation of World War I, there was somewhat of a renewed interest in Reformation theology.

Such academic revivals were far removed from the streets, cabarets, and concert halls of Germany's capital. In the 1920s, Berlin's population reached almost four million, making it the second largest city in Europe. In cultural and intellectual influence, Berlin was remarkable. During the short-lived heyday of 1924-29, before economic collapse came and before another war buried the city in rubble, Berlin enjoyed its golden age of culture. In this period, Fritz Lang made the classic movie *Metropolis* (1926), and Alfred Doeblin wrote his greatest novel, *Berlin Alexanderplatz: The Story of Franz Biberkopf* (1929). Both works reflect the spirit of their times.

Fritz Lang's *Metropolis*

Fritz Lang (1890-1976) was born in Vienna, the only son of a Roman Catholic father and a Jewish convert to Catholicism. Lang rose to become the most prestigious director of Germany's largest film company, Berlin's Universum Film Amt (UFA), in a day when film was Germany's second major industry.[315] In 1926 the UFA produced Lang's *Metropolis*. The film remains as "a great cinematic document of German expressionism."[316]

---
312 John Brose and Kathleen Kerr, *Berlin* (Berlin: H. Hcenernann. 1969), 6.
313 Heick, *A History of Christian Thought*, vol. 2, 234.
314 Wolf von Eckardt and Sander L. Gilman, *Bertolt Brecht's Berlin: A Scrapbook of the Twenties* (Garden City: Anchor Press/Doubleday, 1975), 43.
315 Frederick W. Ott, *The Films of Fritz Lang*, (Secaucus, New Jersey: Citadel Press, 1979), 18.
316 Ott, *The Films of Fritz Lang*, 124.

Seeing the New York skyline on a 1924 trip to America had inspired Lang's vision of the futuristic metropolis, while Flemish Renaissance painter Pieter Brueghel's *Tower of Babel* (1563) was the model for the movie's Tower of Babel. The film's most powerful visuals center around the city skyline with its huge futuristic skyscraper. *Metropolis*'s dominating tower has become not only a symbol for the film but a representation for modernism itself.[317] Yet this building in turn is inspired by the Tower of Babel; in her novel *Metropolis*, Lang's wife Thea von Harbou describes the modern building as "this New Tower of Babel."[318]

Maria, the film's prophet-heroine, retells the story of the Tower of Babel for the workers in Metropolis. She adds several details not found in the Bible. She has Babel's leader declare, "Let us build a tower whose summit will touch the skies, and on it we will inscribe: 'Great is the world and its Creator, and great is Man.'" Maria continues, "Those who conceived the idea of this tower could not have built it themselves, so they hired thousands of others to build it for them. But these toilers knew nothing of the dream of those who planned the tower, while those who conceived them did not concern themselves with the workers who built it" (57-9).

In the Biblical account of Babel (Genesis 11:1-9), the people make no mention of the Creator. They ignore God and declare they want to "make a name for ourselves." In *Metropolis*, the focus of the Babel narrative shifts from a problem of human pride over against God to a problem of man's inhumanity to man. In *Metropolis*'s Babel, the few sing "praises," while they suppress the many. The Bible's Babel mentions neither praises nor suppression.

Lang's artistic license with the scriptural text dovetails with the film's concern with industrialization and worker relations. It also fits the religious climate of turn of the century Europe, when materialistic concerns took precedent over spiritual themes.

Outside of the extensive reference to Babel, *Metropolis* contains only two brief Biblical allusions. One is the cry "Moloch!" as the large subterranean machine devours workers (*Met.* 32). In the Bible, Moloch (also spelled Molech) was a deity whose worship included child sacrifice. The Prophet Jeremiah, for example, decried this practice, "They built high places for Baal in the Valley of Ben Hinnom [outside Jerusalem] to sacrifice their sons and daughters to Molech" (Jeremiah 32:35). As ancient Israelites sacrificed their children to Moloch, so *Metropolis*'s leaders sacrificed the workers to the machine.

---

317 As an example of this, the building serves as the cover illustration for Andreas Huyssen's *After the Great Divide: Modernism, Mass Culture, Postmodernism*, (Bloomington: Indiana University Press, 1986).
318 Fritz Lang, *Metropolis*, in Classic Film Script series, (London: Lorrimer Publishing, 1973), p. 75. Subsequent references to van Harbou's narrative or to the film's title frames are from this edition; page numbers are included in parentheses in the body of the text.

The other allusion to Scripture is the cross, a symbol of the crucified Christ (see Colossians 1:20). Several large crosses form a backdrop in the catacombs (reminiscent of early Christian worship in Rome), where Maria carries out her work of encouraging the workers.

Since the Bible was written long before the advent of modern technology, it might be argued that it has little or no connection with Lang's concerns about the use of technology to suppress people. Yet the Scriptures frequently speak against oppression. The book of Exodus, for instance, decries the Egyptian king's oppression of the Israelites. The pharaoh declared to his people, "Come, we must deal shrewdly with them [the Israelites]," and so the Egyptians "put slave masters over them to oppress them with forced labor" (Exodus 1:10, 11). Whether the tool of oppression is a whip or sophisticated technology, it runs against the grain of Scripture.

On the one hand, *Metropolis* evidences a distrust of technology. On the other, Lang utilized the most advanced technology to create the film. The film's solution to the challenge of technology was the heart acting as mediator between the brain and the hands. To that end, Fritz Lang made use of a number of Biblical subjects, in particular the story of the Tower of Babel.

Alfred Doeblin's *Berlin Alexanderplatz*

Alfred Doeblin (1878-1957) was born of Jewish parentage in Stettin, Pomerania. At age ten, he moved with his family to Berlin. The city would inspire the physician-author for much of his literary output, including his greatest book, *Berlin Alexanderplatz: The Story of Franz Biberkopf*.

This novel makes extensive use of what Walter Benjamin first described as the montage technique of inserting a variety of topics into the narrative.[319] The author "cut and pasted" news reports, hit songs, advertising blurbs, children's verses, radio broadcasts, and even the symbols of the various city departments into the text. Such elements made up the world of 1920s Berlin, and they also served to break down the distinction between subject and object.[320]

Among the montage elements Doeblin has incorporated into his epic are a number of Biblical passages and stories. At times he quotes directly from the Bible, while on other occasions he expands on scriptural narrative to fit it directly into his story, as seen, for instance, in his lengthy "Conversation with Job."[321] Doeblin draws from five different

---

319   David B. Dollenmayer, *The Berlin Novels of Alfred Doeblin* (Berkeley: University of California Press, 1988), 69.
320   Wolfgang Kort, *Alfred Doeblin* (New York: Twayne Publishers, 1974), 103.
321   Alfred Doeblin, *Berlin Alexanderplatz: The Story of Franz Biberkopf*, translated by Eugene Jolas, (New York: Continuum, 1992), 183-8. Subsequent references to *Berlin Alexanderplatz* are from this edition and are included

books of the Bible—Genesis, Job, Ecclesiastes, Jeremiah, and Revelation—referring to each of the five books at least twice.

Except for the book of Revelation, all the Biblical books are from the Old Testament. Given Doeblin's Jewish background, the predominance of Old Testament references is not surprising. In 1941 he converted to Roman Catholicism; yet a dozen years before that, we see him drawing rather frequently from a New Testament book. He has gone to the last book of the Bible, and one of its most highly symbolic books.

The whore of Babylon is the one image from Revelation that Doeblin uses, and reuses. The whore of Babylon receives more attention than any other single scriptural subject, surfacing eight times in the course of three hundred pages. Specific reference to Babylon as the "whore" (or "prostitute" in some translations of the Greek *porne*) occurs in Revelation 17:1, 5 and 19:2. She is described as "the great prostitute" (Revelation 17:1).[322] In Scripture, spiritual apostasy is not infrequently pictured as prostitution; through the Prophet Isaiah, for example, God says of the city of Jerusalem (and the people in general), "See how the faithful city has become a harlot! She once was full of justice; righteousness used to dwell in her—but now murderers!" (1:21)

Given its Old Testament connections, given the subject matter, and given the sheer impact of the term "whore of Babylon," it is not surprising that Doeblin should have utilized this image from Revelation. Almost all of the women with whom the protagonist has relations are prostitutes. Women had been Franz Biberkopf's joy; they had also been his undoing.

Once they are gone, he experiences a "rebirth" of sorts, reminiscent of Jesus' assertion that one must be born again to see the kingdom of God (John 3:3). Biberkopf's rebirth, however, comes not from an encounter with the Gospel. Twice he "does not give in" to the Salvation Army's invitation to "come, sinner, to Jesus" and to the "sinners' bench" (*BA* 430, 545). His new birth comes from an encounter with death. The Christian rebirth occurs after one has been brought down (the Law) and then spiritually uplifted (the Gospel). In Biberkopf's rebirth the Gospel side of religion is conspicuous by its absence. The new Franz Biberkopf has let go of his pride and self-sufficiency, but only for a listless existence as assistant doorman in a factory.

Worldviews

Beneath the religious imagery, *Metropolis* and *Berlin Alexanderplatz* express concerns with urbanization, industrialization, and human

---

in the body of the text in parentheses.
322 The term "whore of Babylon," which Doeblin frequently uses, is not found in the book of Revelation. Babylon is identified as the "great prostitute" (17:1; 19:2) and "the Mother of Prostitutes and of the Abominations of the Earth" (17:5).

alienation. In considering the Germany of the 1920s, we are dealing with a secular culture. Yet it was not a culture that had lost all sense of its religious heritage. Lang and Doeblin use Biblical material in a free-wheeling manner, adapting it to fit their purposes. Babel becomes a worker-management problem, not a human-divine one. The whore of Babylon comes to symbolize human relationships, not spiritual apostasy.

Moreover, both Lang's and Doeblin's selections of Biblical motifs is Law-centered, as opposed to being Gospel-oriented. In this, the theology they reflect stands outside the Reformation heritage. Artistically, the two works are modernist, breaking from the realism of the previous century, and innovative, with Lang's work influencing what has become the gargantuan film industry. Theologically, they are in line with rationalistic trends of the nineteenth and the twenty-first century. Although they employ Scripture, it is more for color than for content.

Though distant in space, time, and culture, ancient Babel and Berlin of the 1920s shared common characteristics. Both were mighty cities, flourishing and creative. Both were proud cities on the brink of destruction. In some ways, the distance is not so far at all between Babel and Berlin—nor between Babel and the modern world in general.

THE BIRTH OF THE MODERN: THE NURTURERS

Eighteenth century deism had seemed to remove God from the ongoing affairs of the world, leaving him with the role of Creator, the Watchmaker who has distanced himself from the work of his hands. Nineteenth century Darwinism took matters to the next stage and removed God from the responsibility for creation itself, which could take care of itself. What was left? There was still the field of morality, as passed on, for example, through natural law and language, as in the Ten Commandments. It remained for the nineteenth and twentieth centuries to take language—as in the concept of divine revelation—from the realm of the divine.

In the new order, man would become the creator and art the medium for conveying the truths of his creation. Instead of an ultimate reality, behind and beyond the human creative activity there is an empty universe. Modernist writers would shake up the language in new ways, just as their contemporaries—e.g., Picasso—were to do with the visual arts. What took place in the early decades of the twentieth century involved both sides of the English Channel, as exemplified in the Bloomsbury group in London, Weimar artists in Berlin, and the so-called Lost Generation of Americans in Paris. Indeed, modernism was a trans-Atlantic blend of American and European innovation. Two American expatriates did much to nurture the movement.

Gertrude Stein

Gertrude Stein (1874-1946) grew up in Oakland, California and went on to study psychology under William James at Radcliffe and medicine at Johns Hopkins. She went to Paris, where she lived with her brother Leo, before taking up residence with her lifelong companion Alice B. Toklas (1877-1967). Gertrude and Leo were among the first to collect the works of experimental painters such as Picasso (who painted her portrait), Matisse, and Braque. Her literary and artistic judgments were revered, and offhand remarks could make or destroy reputations.

Her only book to reach a wide public audience was *The Autobiography of Alice B. Toklas* (1933), actually Stein's own autobiography. Her interest in feminism is evident in the opera *The Mother of Us All* (1947). Much of Stein's work is too tortuous and obscure for general readers, for whom she remains essentially the author of the line "A rose is a rose is a rose is a rose."

Rather than speaking in terms of subjects and objects, Stein's words become the thing itself, the meaning. *Tender Buttons* (1914), subtitled *Objects Food Rooms*, is a series of still lifes of common everyday *objects* with subheadings such as: a box, a piece of coffee, Mildred's umbrella, a red stamp, a plate; *food*: roastbeef, sugar, apple, lunch; chicken. A sampling of the work speaks for itself; under the section entitled Objects is the subheading "Shoes": "A shallow hole rose on red, a shallow hole in and in this makes ale less. It shows shine."[323] The next section, "A Dog," says: "A little monkey goes like a donkey that means to say that means to say that more sighs last goes. Leave with it. A little monkey goes like a donkey" (26).

As Picasso took apart the image—deconstructed it—and then reconstructed it, Stein did with language. We are not left with coherent thought, but with imagery that jars our senses. The message? The reader must decide. A 1914 *Chicago Tribune* review described this "product" of Stein, who is portrayed as "the high Priestess of the New Artists, the Cubists and Futurists": "Miss Stein's followers believe that she has added a new dimension to literature. Scoffers call her writings a mad jumble of words, and some of them suspect that she is having a sardonic joke at the expense of those who profess to believe in her."[324]

Tender Buttons carries fragmentation and abstraction beyond the limits of intelligibility. Language is capable of conveying a series of impressions, images, but can it ever convey more than that? For Stein that seemed to be sufficient.

---

[323] Gertrude Stein, *Tender Buttons: Objects Food Rooms* (New York: Claire Marie, 1914), 26. Subsequent references to this work indicate the page references indicate the page references in parathesis.
[324] As quoted in Michael J. Hoffman, *The Development of Abstractionism in the Writings of Gertrude Stein* (Philadelphia: University of Pennsylvania Press, 1965), 175.

> When asked by a University of Chicago student about the meaning of "a rose is a rose is a rose is a rose," she replied that words in poetry had become "just worn out literary words." . . . Now you have seen hundreds of poems about roses and you know in your bones that the rose is not there . . . Now listen! I'm no fool. I know that in daily life we don't go around saying "is a . . . is . . . is." Yes, I'm no fool; but I think that in that line the rose is red for the first time in English poetry for a hundred years.[325]

The continuous present and the concept of beginning over and over again are key to Stein's work and to her "instructional" book *How to Write*. Disrupting ordinary syntax, Stein fills over 400 pages with plays on words, repetitions, non sequiturs, and any device that will run counter to linear thought, grammar, and syntax. For Stein, grammar is more felt than planned. The traditional use of grammar and words has become stale and needs to be shaken up:

> Against sentences. The whole idea of sentences is that they are with it. The whole sentence is that they come with and then. With and then with and then they may with and then . . . A sentence may help. Think of a sentence peacefully.
>
> This is one sentence.[326]

Amid such ungrammatical grammar and sliced up sentences, Stein includes sentences that do make sense. They seem to spell out her approach to language as art.

Art—whether spoken, painted, or written—was Stein's religion. If there is something beyond the impression, the image, it is not for us to know. According to one biographer, Stein "rejected Christianity as a fairytale and felt that the advantage of her own religion was that 'when a Jew dies he is dead.'"[327] The Hebrew Scriptures, of course, were the original basis of Judaism, and, in spite of what Gertrude Stein thought, they do teach a life to come, as expressed, for example, in Daniel 12:2: "Multitudes who sleep in the dust of the earth will awake: some to everlasting life, others to shame and everlasting contempt." When Stein was near death, before being taken into the operating room, she asked Alice Toklas, "What is the answer?"

When Alice remained silent, Gertrude, quoting herself, said, "In that case What is the question?"[328] These were her last words.

Ezra Pound

Ezra Pound (1885-1972) attended the University of Pennsylvania, where he distinguished himself as a linguist. At the age of twenty-three

---

325 As quoted in Janet Hobhouse, *Everybody Who Was Anybody: A Biography of Gertrude Stein* (New York: G. P. Putnam's Sons, 1975), 185-6.
326 Gertrude Stein, *How to Write* (Los Angeles: Sun and Moon, 1995), 160-1. Pages of subsequent quotes from this work are indicated in parentheses.
327 Hobhouse, *Everybody Who Was Anybody*, 141-2.
328 Hobhouse, *Everybody Who Was Anybody*, 230.

he went to Europe. There he came to know Gertrude Stein and help promote the work of Yeats, Joyce, Hemingway, and Eliot, whose *Waste Land* he edited. Pound not only promoted the careers of other writers, but he himself was an influential theorist and writer. In 1912, he was involved in forming the Imagist Movement.

Following World War I, Pound published poetry, including the first of the *Cantos*, the major poetic work of his life. During World War II, Pound made pro-Fascist radio broadcasts and was detained by U.S. forces for treason in 1945. He was initially held at Pisa, where he wrote his much-acclaimed *Pisan Cantos,* part of his grand life work *The Cantos*.

Pound summarized the essence of Imagism:

1. Direct treatment of the "thing" whether subjective or objective.
2. To use absolutely no word that does not contribute to the presentation.
3. As regarding rhythm: to compose in the sequence of the musical phrase, not in sequence of a metronome.[329]

"Only emotion endures," concludes Pound (69). His most famous poem, the two-line "In a Station of the Metro," is the best example of his Imagism, creating a mental picture:

> The apparition of these faces in the crowd;
>
> Petals on a wet, black bough.[330]

As his Imagism parallels Stein's thought, so Pound's book entitled *ABC of Reading* (1934) is a counterpart of Stein's *How to Write*. Both deal with the study of literature. Both employ disjunction and break down old forms. One critic said of *ABC* that it "reads like the comments of an ex-schoolmaster who has been bereft of his senses. . . ."[331]

In *ABC*, Pound chastises those who would let literature become stagnant:

> Good writers are those who keep the language efficient. That is to say, keep it accurate, keep it clear . . .
>
> Language is the main means of human communication. If an animal's nervous system does not transmit sensations and stimuli, the animal atrophies.
>
> If a nation's literature declines, the nation atrophies and decays. (32)

In his poetry, Pound put his literary theories into practice. Because of numerous insertions of foreign languages and allusions to history and

---

329 Ezra Pound, "A Retrospect," in Peter Faulkner, *The English Modernist Reader, 1910—1930* (Iowa City: University of Iowa Press, 1986), 59. Pages of subsequent references to this work are indicated in the text of the essay. See also Erza Pound, *ABC of Reading* (New York: New Directions, 1987).
330 Ezra Pound, *Selected Poems* (New York: New Directions, 1957), 35.
331 William Van O'Connor, *Ezra Pound* (Minneapolis: University of Minnesota Press, 1963), 41.

mythology, his *Cantos* make for difficult reading.

> Zeus lies in Ceres' bosom
>
> Taishan is attended of loves
>
> under Cythera, before sunrise
>
> and he said: Hay aqui mucho catolicismo—
>
> (sounded catholi*thi*smo)
>
> y muy poco reliHion."[332]

As this little section indicates, the Cantos are dense with allusions to classical mythology, beginning with Zeus, the Greek king of the gods. The reference to Christianity is negative: "There is much Catholicism here—and very little religion." Pound was not a Christian; James Joyce's "*Ulysses*, for him had ended the 'Christian Era.'"[333] Rather, he looked to the East, in particular to Confucius, for resources for his writing and for spiritual insight.

His fascination with the esoteric blended into occultism. Like his mentor Yeats, Pound "drew upon the 'demonic images' of the occult."[334] Moreover, Pound's esoteric interests and search for the ideal government found him in league with Mussolini and making frequent anti-Semitic outbursts in his radio broadcasts, *Ezra Pound Speaking*. Like much of Pound's life and work, his alignment with Fascism and anti-Semitism remain the source of ongoing debate.

Ezra Pound exemplifies the many-faceted turns that modernism's artist as creator might take. If truth is relative, everything becomes arbitrary. Having isolated himself from traditional forms and faith, Pound set his own course. Assailed by "guilt and remorse at the shape his life had taken,"[335] he looked back and wondered, "Shall two know the same thing in their knowing?"[336]

THE BIRTH OF THE MODERN: THE POPULARIZERS

It remained for other writers to popularize the nascent modernist movement. While there were many, two of them—T. S. Eliot and Ernest Hemingway—are of special interest in our study, as they represent not only modernism, but also two different responses to the movement.

---

332 Ezra Pound, *The Cantos of Ezra Pound* (New York: New Directions, 1934), 95.
333 Dennis Brown, *Intertextual Dynamic within the Literary Group—Joyce, Lewis, Pound and Eliot: The Men of 1914* (London: Macmillan, 1990), 109.
334 Timothy Materer, *Modernist Alchemy: Poetry and the Occult* (Ithaca and London: Cornell University Press, 1995), 50.
335 Peter Ackroyd, *T. S. Eliot: A Life* (New York: Simon and Schuster, 1984), 330.
336 Hugh Kenner, *The Pound Era* (Berkeley and Los Angeles: University of California Press, 1971), 561.

T. S. Eliot

Thomas Stearns Eliot (1888-1965) was born in St. Louis and studied at Harvard. In 1910, he moved to France and in 1914 went to England where he worked as an editor until his death. In Europe, Eliot met Ezra Pound, who mentored him and helped get him published. Eliot's first major poem, considered the first modernist masterpiece in English, was *The Love Song of J. Alfred Prufrock* (1915). Together with *The Waste Land* (dedicated to Pound, 1922), it established his international reputation; the latter is often considered the twentieth century's most influential poetic work. Eliot's conversion to Anglo-Catholicism in 1927 shaped all his subsequent creations. His plays include *Murder in the Cathedral* (1935), which treats the martyrdom of Thomas Becket. He won the Nobel Prize in 1948.

Written two years before his conversion, *The Hollow Men* breathes a spirit of desolation, despair, and death. The hue throughout the poem is steely gray, unrelenting in its cold, hard hopelessness. Eliot uses words such as hollow, old, meaningless, broken, death, violent, solemn, fading, alone, dying, lost, empty, shadow, descent . . . The poem begins:

> *A penny for the Old Guy*
>
> We are the hollow men
>
> We are the hollow men
>
> . . . .
>
> Shape without form, shade without colour,
>
> Paralysed force, gesture without motion;[337]

Like Stein, Eliot breaks the rules of grammar, yet all is clear and intelligible. The style is terse—minimalist—leaving more unsaid than is said. For Eliot there is no cheery rose-is-a-rose, no economic or political system to turn to. The poem's last section begins with a nursery rhyme:

> Here we go round the prickly pear
>
> Prickly pear prickly pear
>
> Here we go round the prickly pear
>
> At five o'clock in the morning.

Eliot ends the poem with sentence fragments and a rewording of the child's verse:

> For Thine is the Kingdom
>
> For Thine is
>
> Life is
>
> For Thine is the

---

[337] T. S. Eliot, *The Complete Poems and Plays 1909-1950* (New York: Harcourt, Brace and World, 1952), 56. Subsequent references to *The Hollow Men* are from this edition.

> This is the way the world ends
> This is the way the world ends
> This is the way the world ends
> Not with a bang but a whimper.

The contrast between the nursery rhyme and the somber subject matter could not be stronger. Eliot surpassed Pound and Stein in being able to jolt the language and still convey the message.

The despair Eliot articulated about the world was only underscored by his marriage to Vivien, whose mental illness has become legendary. In the dogmas of the Christian faith, he found a source of discipline for the emotions.

Following his conversion, Eliot sought to enlist the form of modernism in the service of historic Christianity. Already in his essay "Tradition and the Individual Talent" (1919), Eliot had concluded that artists must be responsible to something outside themselves: "No poet, no artist of any art, has his complete meaning alone."[338] Eliot shows how present and past interact and influence each other. It is necessary to take from the past. Only by immersing himself in the stream of tradition and losing himself to the work at hand, can the poet escape from himself and rise above individual personality to produce something of universal significance.

Eliot's "Religion and Tradition" (1935) articulates the role of religion in the arts. Just as an artist needs to move outside his own limited world into a larger literary tradition, so that very tradition needs to be set against a standard outside itself: "The 'greatness' of literature cannot be determined solely by literary standards.... We have tacitly assumed, for some centuries past, that there is *no* relation between literature and theology."[339] Eliot is not advocating that literature needs to make direct theological statements. Rather, he is saying that one's worldview necessarily undergirds and shapes any work. The problem with the contemporary, asserts Eliot, is not that it is immoral or even amoral:

> It is simply that it repudiates, or is wholly ignorant of, our most fundamental and important beliefs; and that in consequence its tendency is to encourage its readers to get what they can out of life while it lasts, to miss no 'experience' that presents itself and to sacrifice themselves, if they make any sacrifice at all, only for the sake of tangible benefits to others in this world either now or in the future.[340]

Some of his poetry is up front in its presentation of Christian themes. *Ash Wednesday* (1930) blends Roman Catholic liturgical phraseology

---
338 T. S. Eliot, "Tradition and Individual Talent," in *Selected Essays* (New York: Harcourt, Brace and World, 1964), 4.
339 Eliot, "Religion and Literature," in *Selected Essays*, 343.
340 Eliot, "Religion and Literature," 354.

with scriptural terminology, in what is widely regarded as an account of Eliot's own journey to faith:

> Pray for us sinners now and at the hour of our death
> Pray for us now and at the hour of our death.
>
> Lord, I am not worthy
> Lord, I am not worthy
>
> But speak the word only.[341]

In other works—*Four Quartets* (1935-42)—the theological theme is set in broader and less recognizable terminology. The work is structured around the four seasons and four medieval elements (earth, air, fire, water). The poem is difficult as Eliot attempts what is humanly impossible, short of divine inspiration, that is, to express the infinite in human language.

Conquering time goes hand in hand with the struggle to conquer words. Eliot turns to Jesus, the incarnate Word (John 1:1), who met the devil's temptations:

> . . .   the Word in the desert
> Is most attacked by voices of temptation
> . . .
>
> Love is itself unmoving,
> Only the cause and end of the movement,
> Timeless, and undesiring
> Except in the aspect of time
> Caught in the form of limitation
> Between unbeing and being. (122)

Eliot is evidently referring to Christ, the God-Man: the beginning and the end (Revelation 1:8), the author and finisher (Hebrews 12:2), the love that breaks through our human condition (1 John 4:16). Of the modernists, Eliot is almost unique in his spiritual journey.[342] Rather than break with his Christian heritage, he revisited it. His religion became Anglo-Catholicism, a return to the religion of England before the time of Henry VIII and the English Reformation, a strain running through centuries and never entirely extinguished. For Eliot, it was not simply a matter of tradition for tradition's sake: "Tradition by itself is not enough . . . Most 'defenders of tradition' are mere conservatives, unable to

---
341 Eliot, *The Complete Poems*, 61-3.
342 Among writers of Eliot's generation or slightly earlier or later, Gerard Manley Hopkins (1844-89), whose work was not published until 1918; G. K. Chesterton (1874-1936); J. R. R. Tolkien (1892-1973); C. S. Lewis (1898-1963); and W. H. Auden (1907-73) stand as other notable converts to Christianity.

distinguish between the permanent and the temporary, the essential and the accidental."[343]

Eliot's life is a reminder that even after the centuries-long waves of religious wars, the Enlightenment and rationalism, deism, Romantic pantheism, Darwinism, skepticism, and art-for-art's sake had washed over the Western world, Christianity was not dead. Two British writers in particular, J. R. Tolkien (1892-1973) and C. S. Lewis (1898-1963), were to exemplify that. Their works such as *The Lord of the Rings* and *The Chronicles of Narnia* reached vast audiences on both sides of the Atlantic—in print and later in film.

Ernest Hemingway

Raised in the Chicago suburb of Oak Park, Ernest Hemingway (1898-1961) is said not only to have used the English language, but to have "reshaped and changed it."[344] His mastery of the short declarative sentence is unparalleled. Knowing both Pound and Stein in Paris, he took the concept of artist as painter and innovator and displayed it to a wider audience, so that more than half a century after his death his books continue to sell in the millions.

In his *Nick Adams Stories*, Hemingway describes the relation between the written word and visual art: "He wanted to write like Cézanne painted. Cézanne started with all the tricks. Then he broke the whole thing down and built the real thing. It was hell to do . . . You could do it if you could fight it out. If you'd lived right with your eyes."[345] Hemingway himself spent a great deal of time studying painting, especially Cézanne and painters after him. From them he learned to extract the essential elements that evoke emotions. Hemingway learned the tricks and used them to elicit an emotional response, as in the following juxtaposition describing World War I action:

> Nick sat against the wall of the church where they had had dragged him to be clear of machine-gun fire in the street. Both legs stuck out awkwardly. He had been hit in the spine. His face was sweaty and dirty. The sun shone on his face. The day was very hot . . . Two Austrians dead lay dead in the rubble in the shade of the house. Up the street were other dead. Things were getting forward into the town. It was going well.[346]

"Writing at its best is a lonely life," stated Hemingway.[347] Writing was lonely and so were his stories. They reveal a loneliness that is ever on the brink of despair. The loneliness of Hemingway's personal life and

---
343 T. S. Eliot, *After Strange Gods: A Primer of Modern Heresy* (London: Faber and Faber, 1934), 62.
344 Roger Jaynes, "Rethinking Hemingway," *Milwaukee Journal*, December 2, 1984.
345 As quoted in Raymond S. Nelson, *Hemingway: Expressionist Artist* (Ames: Iowa State University Press, 1979), vi.
346 Ernest Hemingway, "A Very Short Story," in *The Short Stories of Ernest Hemingway* (New York: Charles Scribner's Sons, 1966), 139.
347 "Ernest Hemingway Reads," audio tape (New York: HarperCollins, 1965).

of his work is reflective of his personal loss of faith. With a grandfather who was a good friend of the evangelist Dwight L. Moody and a father who had considered being a missionary, Hemingway grew up to resent the Christian faith, referring to it as "that ton of s___ we are all fed when we are young."[348]

Hemingway's use of short, staccato-like conversations underscores the feeling of isolation. In "Hills like White Elephants," Hemingway has two characters sitting in a Spanish train station and talking. The conversation between "the American" and "the girl with him" is typical:

> The girl looked at the bead curtain. "They've painted something on it," she said. "What does it say?"
>
> "Anis del Toro. It's a drink."
>
> "Could we try it?"
>
> The man called "Listen" through the curtain. The woman came out from the bar.
>
> "Four reales."
>
> "We want two Anis del Toro."
>
> . . .
>
> "I wanted to try this new drink. That's all we do, isn't it—look at things and try new drinks?"
>
> "I guess so."

Without naming it, they eventually turn to the topic of whether or not to have an abortion:

> "I know you wouldn't mind it, Jig. It's really not anything. It's just to let the air in."
>
> The girl did not say anything.
>
> "I'll go with you and I'll stay with you all the time. They just let the air in and then it's all perfectly natural."
>
> "Then what will we do afterward?"
>
> "We'll be fine afterward. Just like we were before."[349]

This was the empty life of the Lost Generation, so named by Gertrude Stein who together with Alice B. Toklas was godmother for Hemingway's first child. Mere civility, as Brett Ashley says in Hemingway's first novel *The Sun Also Rises*, was "sort of what we have in place of God." The book's title comes from Ecclesiastes, "The sun rises and the sun sets, and hurries back to where it rises" (1:5), a symbol of the empty repetitious nature of life without God.

> "Oh, Jake," Brett said, "we could have had such a damned good time good time together."

---

348 As quoted in Daniel Pawley, "Ernest Hemingway: Tragedy of an Evangelical Family," *Christianity Today*, November 23, 1984: 24.
349 Hemingway, "Hills like White Elephants," in *Short Stories of Ernest Hemingway*, 273-5.

Ahead was a mounted policeman in khaki directing traffic. He raised his baton. The car slowed suddenly pressing Brett against me.

"Yes," I said. "Isn't it pretty to think so?"[350]

The Modernists

Paralleling modern expressionist painting, the modernists injected into their art unique and at times disturbing and difficult elements of form. Each of our modernist writers represents a different branch of the movement. Stein characterizes the modern concept of art as religion. Pound is representative of modernism's spiritual turn toward the East. Hemingway wrote and lived what can well be called modernism's nihilism. Eliot came to represent the relatively few who held to the traditional culture and faith of the West.

THE POSTMODERN WORLD

As secular ideologies grow in influence, so do the results of that worldview, making the religious wars of generations past pale by comparison. Notes Vox Day:

> The total body count for the ninety years between 1917 and 2007 is approximately 148 million dead at the bloody hands of fifty-two atheists [most notably Joseph Stalin and Mao Tse-tung], three times more than all the human beings killed by war, civil war, and individual crime in the entire twentieth century combined. The historical record of collective atheism is thus 182,716 times worse than Christianity's most infamous misdeed, the Spanish Inquisition.[351]

In the West, throughout the twentieth century, the trend toward secularization continues, as evidenced in the world of academia and beyond.

Language and Truth

The twentieth century saw language undergo a phase of tremendous experimentation and innovation. Martin Luther King, Jr. used the power of the written and spoken word in the cause of civil rights. Winston Churchill used it to inspire the British people to their finest hour. For Adolf Hitler—as well as other totalitarians, politicians, and mass marketers—language became a tool for propaganda. Stirring up emotions, rather than expressing truth, became the goal of language. Following World War II, we have been living in the so-called postmodern world, in which the hope of a unified system of knowledge has given way to fragmentation of knowledge and disillusionment with the very ideas of truth and reality.

---

350 Ernest Hemingway, *The Sun Also Rises* (New York: Charles Scribner's Sons, 1954), 247.
351 Vox Day, *The Irrational Atheist: Dissecting the Unholy Trinity of Dawkins, Harris, and Hitchens* (Dallas: Benbella, 2008), 240.

Literature and Philosophy

"A poet's function," wrote poet-philosopher Paul Valéry in 1939, "is not to experience the poetic state: that is a private affair. His function is to create it in others."[352] The experience of the poetic state now becomes the "private affair" of the individual reader or viewer, and much of today's literary criticism emphasizes the reader response. This is nothing new; people have always reacted to works of art. What has changed is the emphasis on the response.

This emphasis on reader response is but one of many schools of literary criticism. Other critical approaches are formalist, biographical, psychological, historical, sociological, Marxist, feminist, mythological, and deconstructionist. Not only English majors, but all college students taking mandatory literature classes encounter a diversity of critical approaches. The deconstructionist approach breaks a composition into its elementary components. Along with reader-response, this approach is evidence of what we might call the fragmentation of literary studies; the word "fragmentation" fits much of what is happening in academia and elsewhere.

The literary canon has also become more diversified, and the very notion of canon has become suspect. As an example of this, eighteenth-century women writers (such as Sarah Scott and Charlotte Smith) who were unread and perhaps not even in print thirty or forty years ago are now the subject of university literature courses. The study of minority and lifestyle literature seems to have reached a balance with the classics—Shakespeare and Milton. Diversification along with fragmentation, then, is another term that describes current literary studies.

Ludwig Wittgenstein

A prime example of the literary-philosophical connection is Ludwig Wittgenstein (1889-1951), generally considered the premier philosopher of the past century. In his early work, *Tractatus Philosophicus,* Wittgenstein contended that language can be broken down into its simpler components and analyzed as it corresponds to the real world. Arguing that we cannot speak of what we do not know, he rejected metaphysics and asserted we can only speak in a meaningful way about what is verifiable.[353] Later, in *Philosophical Investigations,* Wittgenstein critiqued his earlier work for its simple one-on-one correspondence between words and reality, while maintaining his basic ideas,

Wittgenstein's philosophy is closely connected to the arts. He has been called the philosopher of poets, composers, playwrights, and

---

352 Paul Valéry, *Poetry and Abstract Thought*, in Adams, *Critical Theory since Plato,* 912.
353 For an analysis of Wittgenstein's thought, see Donald Hudson, *Ludwig Wittgenstein: The Bearing of His Philosophy upon Religious Belief* (Richmond: John Knox, 1968).

novelists, and parts of his *Tractatus* have even been set to music. "We speak as we do," he said, "because of what we do."[354] Capturing the "big picture" or a deeper something, for Wittgenstein was not an option. What we have is what we talk about. Do not look for anything beyond, behind, or beneath—including religious truths. Other postmodern philosophers such as Richard Rorty (1931-2007) reject the idea of objective Truth (as *the* Truth with a capital T) but look for truth in what works, especially in social solidarity.

Linguistics and Theology

Theology was once considered the queen of the sciences. Today that is no longer the case. Its displacement goes back at least in part to the rise of modern philology in the nineteenth and twentieth centuries. With the expansion of the British Empire into India, European scholars took their first good look at Sanskrit. One of the outcomes of that encounter was the discovery that Sanskrit predated Hebrew.[355] For many this came as a shock; they had supposed that Hebrew was the original language given by God in Eden, even though the Bible itself does not make that assertion. Earnest Renan had been quick to see the implications of this discovery. It meant not only that questions would arise concerning the place of Biblical faith, but it also put philology at the center of the sciences. Edward Said notes:

> The job of philology in modern culture (a culture Renan calls philological) is to continue to see reality and nature clearly, thus driving out supernaturalism, and to continue to keep pace with discoveries in the physical sciences.... There is an unmistakable aura of power about the philologist.[356]

Renan had used philology to argue that the Semitic languages were only partially developed and on a lower level than the Indo-European family of languages that included Sanskrit and the modern languages of Europe. In this way, asserts Said, philology became a tool of European colonialism as well as undermining confidence in the Bible.

When applied to Biblical scholarship, linguistics has generally been less than kind. The most severe attacks on the Bible—both Old and New Testaments—have not come from without but from linguistic specialists at colleges, universities, and seminaries within Christian lands.

An especially destructive use of linguistic studies has arisen with the development of higher criticism. This is distinguished from lower criticism, which seeks to establish the precise reading of Scripture's Hebrew

135

---

354 Michael Peters and James Marshall, "Terry Eagleton: Wittgenstein as Philosophical Modernist (*and* Postmodernist)," <http://faculty.ed.uiuc.edu/burbules/ncb/syllabi/materials/Eagleton.html>
355 See Edward W. Said, *Orientalism* (New York: Vintage, 1979), 123-48; Rosane Rocher, "Discovery of Sanskrit by Europeans," in E. F. K. Koerner and R. E. Asher, ed., *Concise History of the Language Sciences: From the Sumerians to the Cognitivists.* Cambridge: UK, 1995), 188-91.
356 Said, *Orientalism,* 132.

and Greek texts; lower criticism continues to hold the Biblical text in high regard, neither questioning its integrity nor arguing with its content. Higher criticism sets itself above the Biblical text, as it would any secular manuscript. Its aim is to determine the original document(s) beneath what it considers a text free of divine involvement. A particular branch of higher criticism is form criticism, as espoused by Rudolph Bultmann (1884-1976), who doubted the historical reliability of the New Testament and sought to "demythologize" it.[357] Bultmann claimed the Biblical picture of Christ "is incredible to men and women today because for them the mythical world is a thing of the past."[358] Others would take up where Bultmann left off.

Along with linguistics, comparative historical research plays a role in contemporary Bible studies. This is a two-sided coin. On the one hand, some scholars—for example, the Jesus Seminar—have used their study of ancient manuscripts to question the New Testament canon. Others have found in the same research evidence of the reliability of the Biblical canon.[359]

"The truth will set you free"

The ongoing argument over the Bible's reliability involves much more than academic debate. It has to do with the Bible's concept of truth. At his civil trial before the Roman magistrate, Jesus testified about himself, "[F]or this reason I was born, and for this I came into the world, to testify to the truth. Everyone on the side of truth listens to me." To which, Pontius Pilate gave his famous reply, "What is truth?" (John 18:37-8)

For asking that question, in *The Antichrist* (§ 46), Nietzsche called Pilate "a solitary figure worthy of honor" and his question "the only saying that has any value" in the New Testament.[360] In "Truth and Falsity in an Ultramoral Sense," Nietzsche anticipates postmodernism and asks, "What therefore is truth?"[361]

From the Biblical perspective, truth is more than words. It is a way of life. The Bible's reliability—indeed, its inerrancy—stands up under the scrutiny of linguistic and historical analysis. But ultimately, it is a matter of faith.

The Bible, then, offers the solution to the relation between language and truth. It comes through a relationship with Jesus, who is God in the

---

357 See Michael Parsons, "Bultmann," in *New 20th-Century Encyclopedia of Religious Knowledge,* second edition, J. D. Douglas, ed. (Grand Rapids: Baker, 1991); Walter A. Maier, *Form Criticism Reexamined* (St. Louis: Concordia, 1973).
358 As quoted in Wilbert R. Gawrisch, *Who Is Jesus Christ?: Current Issues in Christology* (Milwaukee: Northwestern, 2002), 28.
359 See Philip Jenkins, *Hidden Gospels: How the Search for Jesus Lost Its Way* (New York: Oxford University Press, 2001).
360 See David Bentley Hart on Nietzsche, Jesus, and Pilate, March 30, 2010, http://veraicona.org/?s=pilate
361 Friedrich Nietzsche, "Truth and Falsity in an Ultramoral Sense," 636.

flesh, and who brings to this benighted world forgiveness, life, and salvation. Christ declared: "If you hold to my teaching you are really my disciples. Then you will know the truth and the truth will set you free" (John 8:31-32).

The opposite of truth is not intellectual error, but moral failing. Jesus continues, "[E]veryone who sins is a slave to sin" (John 8:34). One knows truth by trusting Christ; it cannot be fully discerned in a test-tube, a library, or word studies. Theologian John Philip Koehler elucidates: "The doctrine of our salvation is not a subtle system of connections of thought which we can prove to another by explaining to him the connections. It is rather a wonderful revelation of the wonderful mighty works of God, to which we testify with the power of the Holy Spirit."[362]

The Decline of Western Christianity

The trend toward specialization in Western learning has been productive of advances in many fields, but it has also resulted in an occasionally alarming inability to see the big picture. One wonders how much longer Western civilization can hold together without the overarching Christian worldview that for so long furnished its most fundamental values and attitudes. What happens when the postmodern infatuation with deconstruction and randomness takes its place? In the words of W. B. Yeats, "Things fall apart; the centre cannot hold."[363]

Waning of the British Empire

Christianity had been the main spiritual force animating the English people during the most glorious years of their history. And it is not merely coincidental that the rise and fall of the British Empire should parallel the rise and fall of English Reformation faith. In describing the Empire as it approached its pinnacle, Lawrence James spells out the factors that contributed to British greatness (in mid nineteenth century), concluding,

> There was also, and this was continually announced from the pulpit and set down in tracts and editorials, that inner strength and purposefulness that individuals derived from a Christian faith which set a high store on personal integrity, hard work and a dedication to the general welfare of mankind.[364]

For many today, allusions to empire and religion in the same breath bring to mind everything they find wrong with the world. It is striking that England's chief claim to fame in the late twentieth century should fall into

---
362 Joh. Ph. Koehler, *The Epistle of Paul to the Galatians*, translated from the German by E. E. Sauer (Milwaukee: Northwestern, 1957), 80.
363 William Butler Yeats, "The Second Coming," *Selected Poems and Three Plays*, 89.
364 Lawrence James, *The Rise and Fall of the British Empire* (New York: St. Martin's, 1994), 169-70.

the hands of a pop music group called the Beatles, one of whom would envision in song a world bereft of nations and religion:

> Imagine there's no countries
>
> It isn't hard to do
>
> Nothing to kill or die for
>
> And no religion too
>
> Imagine all the people
>
> Living life in peace . . . [365]

Such an imaginary world is not the solution. Rather, it is a matter of what kind of religion we have and what kind of nations we build.

A Look at Statistics

Years of onslaught—both subtle and frontal—have weakened Christianity's hold in the West. Statistics bear this out. According to the comprehensive *World Christian Encyclopedia,* in the past century, in Africa the percentage of Christians has astoundingly increased from 9.2% (1900) to 45.9% (2000).[366] Worldwide, "the total of Christians has grown enormously, from 558 millions in 1900 to 2,000 millions by AD 2000." . . .

> But no-one in 1900 expected the massive defections from Christianity that subsequently took place in Europe due to secularism, in Russia and later Eastern Europe due to Communism, and in the Americas due to materialism. . . .
>
> [E]very year, some 2,765,100 church attenders in Europe and North America cease to be practicing Christians within the 12-month period, an average loss of 7,600 every day.
>
> At the global level, these losses from Christianity in the Western world slightly outweigh the gains in the Third World. . . . In 1900, Christians numbered 34.5% of the world . . . in AD 2000, 33.0%.[367]

North America was long considered a stronghold of Protestant Christianity. In 1900, Protestants accounted for 45.7% of the population; by 2000, that fell to 22.6%.[368] Focusing on the United States, another survey includes the following information:

> Every year more than 4000 churches close their doors compared to just over 1000 new church starts! . . . From 1990 to 2000, the combined membership of all Protestant denominations in the USA declined by almost 5 million members (9.5 percent), while the US population increased by 24 million (11 percent).

---

365 John Lennon, "Imagine," Bagism: John Lennon Discography, <http://www.bagism.com/lyrics/imagine-lyrics.html#Imagine>

366 David B. Barrett, George T. Kurian, and Todd M. Johnson, *World Christian Encyclopedia: A comparative survey of churches and religions in the modern world,* second edition (Oxford and New York: Oxford University Press, 2001), vol. 1, 13.

367 Barrett, *World Christian Encyclopedia,* vol. 1, 3.

368 Barrett, *World Christian Encyclopedia,* vol. 1, 14.

At the turn of the last century (1900), there was a ratio of 27 churches per 10,000 people, as compared to the close of this century (2000) where we have 11 churches per 10,000 people in America![369]

A December 2007 Gallup Poll furnished the following information on shifting patterns: In 1948, 69% of Americans were Protestant, 22% Catholic; in 2007, 51% were Protestant, 23% Catholic.[370] In a period of sixty years, then, American Protestantism has declined by almost 20 percent. If this seems to be a different society than it was sixty years ago, that's because it is.

Implications

The decline of the Western church has many and great implications, such as, for instance, the loss of the concept of work as a God-given vocation. We will touch on three key areas.

One is the foundation of society, the family. The family unit has been weakened in a number of ways: no-fault divorce, single-parents households, the push for same-sex marriages, abortion on demand, and an emphasis on small families. Even from the purely human standpoint, many of the current attitudes toward families are destructive of civilization. Abortion and same-sex unions will not produce the next generation. In Europe, where the birthrate is not sufficient to sustain the population, Muslims (producing large families) are moving in—hence the death of European civilization[371] followed by the Islamization of Europe.[372]

A second area relates to the shift to other worldviews. Besides Christianity, in today's world there are three other dominant ways of looking at the world: (1) Muslim, (2) Eastern (pantheistic-monistic), (3) Secular (humanistic or materialistic). None of these is amiable toward Christianity. Islam's foundational book, the Qur'an, rejects the heart of Christian faith—the triune God along with the incarnation and crucifixion of Christ.[373] The Eastern worldview replaces resurrection with reincarnation and the transcendent God with the notion that we are all part of the divine.[374] A secular worldview discards the spiritual for the physical and denies the very need for divine revelation.[375] All reject Jesus Christ as the Savior of the human race.

---

369 Richard J. Krejcir, "Statistics and Reasons for Church Decline," Schaeffer Institute, http://www.intothyword.org/articles_view.asp?articleid=36557
370 Gallup, Questions and Answers About Americans' Religion, http://www.gallup.com/poll/103459/questions-answers-about-americans-religion.aspx
371 See Patrick J. Buchanan, *The Death of the West: How Dying Populations and Immigrant Invasions Imperil Our Country and Civilization* (New York: Thomas Dunne, 2002.
372 See Robert Spencer, "The Rapid Islamization of Europe," September 18, 2004, http://theroadtoemmaus.org/RdLb/33Rlg/Islm/IslmInEu02.htm; Eugene Girin, "Islam in the City of Light," *Chronicales: A Magazine of American Culture*, August 2012, 40-1.
373 See, for instance, Roland Cap Ehlke, *Speaking the Truth in Love to Muslims* (Milwaukee: Northwestern, 2004).
374 See, for instance, Victor A. R. Raj, *The Hindu Connection: Roots of the New Age* (St. Louis: Concordia, 1995).
375 See, for instance, Herbert Schlossberg, *Idols for Destruction: The Conflict of Christian Faith and American Culture* (Wheaton, IL: Crossway, 1990).

That segues to the third area, which might be termed moral-equivalency. Among the founders of world religions, Jesus is unique. He claims to be God; he performed miracles and arose from the dead; he offers free salvation to all who simply place their trust in him. Christians are not better than anyone else, but their Savior-God is. This does not go over well with a culture that tends to view all religions as equally valid. Many seem to think that the Christian underpinning of the West can be replaced with any other worldview, and society will function just as well or even better. All we need is the right economic system and the right politicians.

Given such mainstream thinking, we can expect that Christianity will get little credit for the achievements of this civilization, as Catherine Millard argues in *The Rewriting of America's History*.[376] On the other hand, there is a mindset ready to hold the churches accountable for all their faults—both real and imagined. Christianity is viewed in an increasingly antagonistic way.

"One of the most traumatic experiences that I, as a new immigrant to the United States of America, faced was the unrelenting and vicious attacks on the practice of the Christian faith here," writes Ohikhaiteme D. Amu, a Christian who with his family migrated from Nigeria. "Hardly a week goes by without another litigation to stop the display of a cross, or saying of prayers, or mentioning God in places the litigants consider government or public places."[377]

Martin Luther noted that there really is no such thing as a Christian country:

> God has ordained two governments: the spiritual, by which the Holy Spirit produces Christians and righteous people under Christ; and the temporal, which restrains the un-Christian and wicked . . .
>
> [T]he world and the masses are and always will be un-Christian, even if they are all baptized and Christian in name. Christians are few and far between . . . Therefore, it is out of the question that there should be a common Christian government over the whole world, or indeed over a single country or any considerable body of people, for the wicked always outnumber the good.[378]

Nevertheless, when scriptural principles infuse a society, the people are blessed. In that dispensation, life was lived under the umbrella of the sacred, and everything from harvests to sicknesses was received as blessings, tests, or punishments from above.

Today life is filtered through a secular lens. Ironically, while claiming the opposite, the secular (literally, of this world) view is more limited than that vision which sees so much more than what is here. Nor is that "so much more" going to be discovered through telescopes or

---

376 Catherine Millard, *The Rewriting of America's History* (Camp Hill, PA: Horizon House, 1991).
377 Ohikhaiteme D. Amu, "Separation of Church and State," unpublished paper, May, 2012.
378 Martin Luther, "Temporal Authority: To What Extent It Should Be Obeyed," *Luther's Works*, vol. 45, (Philadelphia, PA: Fortress Press, 1967), 91.

microscopes. The new order, according to Ferdinand de Saussure, has no pre-existing ideas.[379] Artistic and linguistic relativity belong in the same world as moral relativity. Says one scholar, "It is difficult for modern man, possessed of great respect for science and human reason, to find adequate ground for an absolute theory of right and wrong. All the evidence which commands his respect seems to point away from this to a relative position."[380]

That evidence is not in the human heart, which perceives there must be truth and longs for a morality to live by and an ideal worth dying for, yet cannot find it. Moreover, sound philosophical reasoning as well as Biblical ethics contends against moral relativism.[381] Arguably, the modern aesthetic disposition is nothing more (or less) than an expression of the desire for meaning:

> The importance attributed to art near the end of the eighteenth century has its roots in the decline of theology and the disintegration of theologically legitimated social orders: 'All that is solid melts into the air', as Marx put it in the *Communist Manifesto*. The loss of a nature whose meaning is inherent within it and whose structure is divinely guaranteed leads to a search for other sources of meaning and coherence.[382]

"Always learning but never able to acknowledge the truth" (2 Timothy 3:7)—the search goes on.

141

---

379   Ferdinand de Saussure, *Course in General Linguistics*, in Adams, *Critical Theory since Plato*, 720.
380   S. E. Frost, *Basic Teachings of the Great Philosophers*, (Garden City, NY: Doubleday, 1962), 99.
381   See James Rachels, "Morality Is Not Relative," in Pojman and Vaughn, *Philosophy: The Quest for Truth*, 483-92.
382   Andrew Bowie, *Aesthetics and Subjectivity: From Kant to Nietzsche*, (Manchester: Manchester University Press, 1990), 3.

CONCLUSION: THE END OF AN AGE

While working on this project, I came across a news item that—like a thousand others—confirms my thesis: "A hotel in the United Kingdom has replaced in-room Gideon Bibles with the soft-porn bestseller *Fifty Shades of Grey*. The change was made earlier this month in all 40 guest rooms at the Damson Dene Hotel in the Lake District [birthplace of the Romantic movement] of England."[383] This is the stuff of the modern (or postmodern) mind.

Since the Age of Enlightenment, the Western world has been involved in a shift away from its Christian foundations. Our overview of culture reflects the philosophical and theological changes that have been sweeping through England and the West. This is not to imply that the history of aesthetics is simply a linear progression from "there" to "here." Not everyone who followed Kant in time, for example, necessarily followed all his ideas.

The shift into a materialistic, reason-oriented, and human-centered world is a reality, so that Pierre Bourdieu can correctly speak of today's culture as "that present incarnation of the sacred."[384] The modern fascination with corporeal beauty is but a return to what Augustine had labeled "the lowest beauty," while attraction to the occult and new religions is but an attempt to salvage a sense of the spiritual in a material world.

There is something else involved. In today's world obsessed with the momentary rush of sports, entertainment, pop stars and the internet, everyone is aware of it. It is the matter of flux. Yet amid the flux, remains this constant—the human longing for that which lasts. This is another of the age-old yearnings of the heart that remain in modern and postmodern men and women.

Alongside the general movement away from Christianity, there is another phenomenon. It is the fact that the Christian church and a Christian consciousness have remained—sustained, so to speak, by pools left from the rain. However weakened, Christianity is still present—both as something from which to move away and as a haven to which one might return. That strange amalgam was evident in the "National Day of Prayer and Remembrance" service held at the National Cathedral on September

---

383   British hotel replaces Bibles with 'Fifty Shades of Grey," July 2012, http://travel.usatoday.com/hotels/post/2012/07/british-hotel-replaces-bibles-with-fifty-shades-of-grey/811553/1?csp=twusattravel_sf5231127&sf5231127=1
384   Pierre Bourdieu, *Distinction: A Social Critique of the Judgment of Taste*, translated by Richard Nice (Cambridge, MA: Harvard University Press, 1984), xiii.

14, 2001, three days after the terrorist attacks.[385] The service included readings from the New Testament by Christian clerics, from the Old Testament by a Jewish rabbi, words from the President, a sermon by Billy Graham, and a prayer by a Muslim imam. Given that the Qur'an explicitly rejects the Trinity (even as Judaism rejects Jesus as the Messiah), it was not a prayer to the God of Scripture—yet there it was in the National Cathedral, generic religion in service of the state.

The service also included the singing of Isaac Watts' "O God, Our Help in Ages Past" and Luther's "A Mighty Fortress Is Our God." Throughout the years, there have been many who with deep conviction have followed the likes of Martin Luther and Isaac Watts, of Milton and Bunyan, and still held to such theological basics as the Atonement. The fact that a number of artists and intellectuals—along with so many others—have held on to the faith is an indication that the path away from Christian truths was not an intellectual necessity. None of the movements and writers we have considered has really torn down or disproved the tenets of the faith as, for example, the resurrection of Christ.

Yet this other side no longer represents the mainstream of Western civilization; it becomes ever more reminiscent of the Biblical remnant. From our vantage point two millennia after Christ, we are able to trace a profound shift in civilization as we know it. The shift is clearly evident in art and literature. Ironically, in spite of its powerful impact, the man on the street is probably quite unaware of this change and no doubt indifferent to it.

Christianity's fading in the West is not synonymous with its demise. While Christian faith has become increasingly marginal in the West, it has taken root in other parts of the globe. The majority of Christians in the world today is no longer in the traditional lands of Christendom—Europe and North America. The Gospel is moving on.

For those who remain behind and still have not bowed the knee to Baal (1 Kings 19:18), there is much to do, and there still is time for renewal and revival. Jesus says, "As long as it is day, we must do the work of him who sent me. Night is coming, when no one can work" (John 9:4). We carry on the work—that is, to live for Christ, who has died for us—not with resignation but with joy. And how can it be otherwise? The Creator of the universe has entered this world, become our brother, died for our sins, and risen from death to secure for us forgiveness, salvation, and an eternity in heaven. This is the wonder of the triune God and the glory of the cross of Christ, who transcends all worldly civilizations and has established an everlasting kingdom. He is with us always.

Soli Deo Gloria!

---

[385] See September 14, 2001, National Day of Prayer and Remembrance, http://www.nationalcathedral.org/events/eventTexts/wtc20010914TT.shtml

FOR STUDY AND DISCUSSION

Part 1. The Age of Reformation 1450—1650

1. Review the key persons, events, and movements of the period.
2. How did the Renaissance influence the Reformation?
3. What major religious themes marked the Reformation? What were the great contributions of Martin Luther? (Note especially Romans 1:16-17.)
4. In what ways did the Christian faith interact with science and intellectual life? (See 1 Corinthians 10:31.)
5. In what ways did Christian faith affect the arts—literature, music, painting, etc.?
6. How did the Lutheran Reformation differ from the English Reformation?
7. Where did Protestantism prevail? Roman Catholicism? How did that affect subsequent history?
8. How were the religious wars expressions of both religious and political attitudes?
9. Even when at odds with one another, what common values and beliefs did Europeans share during this period?
10. While representative, *Like a Pelting Rain* is not exhaustive. Comment on other events and persons that you have encountered in reading or studies.

Part 2. The Age of Enlightenment 1650—1800

1. Review the key persons, events, and movements of the period.
2. Define Arminianism and Deism, and note the inroads they made into Protestant theology.
3. What were the main features of the Enlightenment? In what ways are we still living under its influence?
4. How did Enlightenment thought affect the intellectuals and the common people?
5. Review the reasons for and impact of the rise of the novel.
6. Note the changing role of aesthetics during this period. What changes took place in the arts and music?

7. What was Immanuel Kant's "Copernican revolution," and how has it affected thought down to this day?

8. How did the worldwide spread of Christian missions attest to God's grace in the age of Enlightenment? (See Matthew 24:14, Revelation 7:9.)

9. How did Enlightenment ideals and Christian preaching coexist side by side? How was Latitudinarianism a compromise between the two?

10. While representative, *Like a Pelting Rain* is not exhaustive. Comment on other events and persons that you have encountered in reading or studies.

Part 3. The Age of Romanticism 1800--1850

1. Review the key persons, events, and movements of the period.

2. What distinguished Romanticism from the Age of Reason (the Enlightenment)? What common attitudes did both movements have toward Christianity?

3. Distinguish between the earlier and later English Romantic poets. How did the later achieve or fail in their search for transcendence?

4. What were the outstanding features of Romantic music and art?

5. Did American Romanticism significantly differ from the European? If so, in what ways?

6. Comment on Edgar Allan Poe's influence on later writers and literature in general. How does that influence underscore Shelley's notion that poets are the "unacknowledged legislators of the world"?

7. How did Ralph Waldo Emerson and Poe reflect the Romantic spirit? Note their similarities and differences.

8. During the Romantic period Christian churches flourished in the United States. Research and reflect on what stage your church was at during this time.

9. Note the differences between what might be termed a Christian and a secular Romanticism. (Galatians 5:22-23 relates to the place of faith in the emotional life.)

10. While representative, *Like a Pelting Rain* is not exhaustive. Comment on other events and persons that you have encountered in reading or studies.

Part 4. The Victorian Age 1850—1900

1. Review the key persons, events, and movements of the period.
2. This section contains entire chapters devoted to four representative persons: Charles Dickens, Alfred Lord Tennyson, Charles Darwin, and Sarah Orne Jewett. Their lives were very different, yet how were they all children of that age?
3. In what ways do Darwin's ideas continue to influence the world? Reflect on the ongoing creation-evolution debate.
4. How did the Christian faith of Dickens differ from that of his contemporaneous Londoner the great preacher Charles Haddon Spurgeon?
5. How did Tennyson, Robert Browning, and Matthew Arnold attempt to deal with the receding of Christian faith from England?
6. How did New England spirituality (as exemplified by Jewett and others) differ from other parts of America during this period?
7. Comment on the art for art's sake movement of the later nineteenth century.
8. How was the picture of Christianity painted by Oscar Wilde (and other contemporaries) different from that of the Bible? (See 1 Timothy 6:20-21.)
9. What current attitudes toward religion are similar to those of the Victorian Age?
10. While representative, *Like a Pelting Rain* is not exhaustive. Comment on other events and persons that you have encountered in reading or studies.

Part 5. The Age of Modernism and Beyond 1900—the Present

1. Review the key persons, events, and movements of the period.
2. How did the occult beliefs of William Butler Yeats affect his work?
3. Comment on the religious scene in Germany from the time of Luther until the twentieth century.
4. Point out key features of modern music and art. Might we say that the world of aesthetics expanded to include sports and entertainment in general? If so, why?
5. Looking at the cultural shift during the past five centuries, what features stand out most?

6. How has the loss of Christian faith—and with it, values—affected today's society?

7. In addition to T. S. Eliot, C. S. Lewis, and J. R. Tolkien, what other modern Christian artists come to mind? How have they influenced society for the better?

8. Point out major features of postmodernism. Where might Western society be headed in the near future?

9. What signs are there that the Holy Spirit is still active in our communities and throughout the world? What encouragements and confidence do Christians find in the Scriptures which make us "wise for salvation through faith in Christ Jesus" (2 Timothy 3:15)?

10. While representative, *Like a Pelting Rain* is not exhaustive. Comment on other events and persons that you have encountered in reading or studies.

www.ingramcontent.com/pod-product-compliance
Lightning Source LLC
Chambersburg PA
CBHW070109120526
44588CB00032B/1404